WHEN POETS WERE WARRIORS

Casey B. Hough

When Poets Were Warriors

Retrieving a Biblical Vision of Masculinity

B&H Publishing®
Brentwood, Tennessee

Printed in the United States of America

979-8-3845-0068-1

Published by B&H Publishing Group,
Brentwood, Tennessee

Dewey Decimal Classification: 305.31
Subject Heading: JESUS CHRIST—
HUMANITY \ MEN \ MASCULINITY

Cover design and illustration: Faceout Studio, Spencer Fuller. Author photo by Jessica Keevan.

1 2 3 4 5 6 • 28 27 26 25

To Carter, Jude, and Weston.
My prayer is that you would continue to grow into the kind of men that God has called you to be in Christ.
Thank you for your gracious patience with me as a father who's still growing in Christ.

ACKNOWLEDGMENTS

As with any project like this, it would be impossible to acknowledge everyone who has played a role, but alas, I must make a feeble attempt.

First, I want to thank my wife, Hannah. I cannot imagine what kind of man I would be without her. Apart from my salvation in Christ, God has bestowed no greater blessing on my life than my wife. I love you, Honey. May your household rise up to call you blessed (Prov. 31:28)!

Second, I want to thank my children, Carter, Jude, Weston, Eden, and Willow, for their patience with me during this season of life. I love each of you so much. I pray that each of you will learn what it is to grow into the kind of men and women that God has called us to be in Christ.

Third, I want to thank my parents, Ronald and Kay Hough, and my in-laws, Tim and Holly Nicholls. While my dad, Ronald, is with the Lord now, his example still exerts a profound influence on my life. I miss you, Dad, but I am grateful that while we grieve, we do not grieve as those without hope. To my mom, Kay, thank you for pointing me and my brothers to Christ for so many years. To Tim and Holly, thank you for your constant encouragement and the examples you have set for our family. I cannot imagine having a better family. All of you make it easy to come home for the holidays.

Fourth, I want to thank Stuart Sheehan, CEO/ President of World Hope Ministries International. In so many ways, you embody the vision of this book. It is an honor to serve our Lord together as we seek to see the church around the world equipped for every good work in Christ.

Fifth, I must acknowledge my wonderful group of friends. In particular, I'd like to thank Eric Nimtz, Stephen Partain, Bart Salmon, Andrew Brown, Travis Rupp, Dustin Bruce, Dan Darling, Andrew Walker, Josh Wester, Erik Reed, and Dean Inserra. You guys have listened to me drone on and on about this topic for years now. Your insight and encouragement fueled this work, and for that, I am grateful.

Finally, I would like to thank my literary agent, Brad Byrd, with Wadestone Inc., for his advocacy and guidance during this project. I am also grateful to Matthew Hawkins and the team at B&H Publishing. Your patience and persistence were key to getting this project across the finish line.

CONTENTS

Introduction

WHAT KIND OF MAN CRIES?

"Stop crying! Suck it up! Man up! Be a man! You're acting like a girl!" On more than one occasion, I've hollered these types of comments at my sons. I typically did this at sporting events when they would demonstrate some sort of tender emotion. It might have been when they had struck out, walked a batter, missed a layup, or missed a tackle. They would cry. I would scream. They would bite their lip and soldier on. I felt vindicated. I told myself I was raising "real men," but honestly, at the time, I didn't even know what that meant.

My journey to understand what it means to be a Christian man began next to a baseball field dugout. I had pulled one of my sons off to the side to give him a pep talk. He was crying about his performance. I gritted my teeth, looked him in the eyes, and said, "You've got to quit crying. You've got to man up. Men don't cry." I felt like Jimmy Dugan from *A League of Their Own*: "There's no crying in baseball!" This was not a new scene in our story, but something felt different after this encounter. For the first time, I felt like something was wrong. That something wrong was me. It was the last three words of my "conversation" with my son that hung in the air: "Men don't cry." I knew this was wrong. So, why was I saying it?

I am not the first to wrestle with these feelings. In his book, *Cry like a Man: Fighting for Freedom from Emotional Incarceration*, Jason Wilson aptly described the dilemma so many men have found themselves in. He writes, "With all the theories, credos, and misleading mantra—'Man up,' 'No pain, no gain,' not to be outdone by the mother of all misguided intelligence, 'Real mean don't cry'—we have been deceived into suppressing our emotions to impress others; there is simply no room for weakness."[1] Wilson explains how men "from childhood through early puberty then into manhood *have been* conditioned to swallow our pain, expressing little but indifference and detachment about the chaos around us."[2] Wilson goes on in his book to vividly describe this suppression of male emotion as "emotional incarceration." In my case, I was the looming officer making sure my boys didn't get out of line.

After that fateful afternoon next to the dugout, I wish I could say I rushed home for some deep soul-searching, but I didn't. The discomfort I felt did not find a settled place in me, but the disruption sowed enough seeds to bear fruit along the rocky path of my heart, weeks later, while I read through the Gospels. As I worked through Matthew, Mark, and Luke, I encountered the perfect man, Jesus the Nazarene.

This was not my first encounter with Jesus. I grew up learning about Him on Sundays and Wednesdays at my Baptist church and every school day at my private, fundamentalist Baptist academy. I knew a lot about Jesus, even winning the "Best Christian Example" award a few years in a row. That sounds even more impressive considering that I wasn't actually a Christian at the time. But God, in His grace, did not allow me to stay in that condition. In His great mercy, when I was seventeen, God opened my heart to receive the gospel. I was forgiven, made new, born again.

With this new life in Christ came an insatiable desire to learn more about this God who saved me. I read almost everything I could get my hands on. Before my conversion, I'm pretty sure the only book I had actually read from cover to cover was Matt Christopher's *Return of the Home Run Kid*. But that changed when God redeemed me. My love for reading came out of nowhere, and my favorite author outside of the Bible became (and remains) John Piper.

The first sermon I ever remember really listening to was a Piper sermon on marriage and the glory of God. It was glorious. I wore out that cassette tape (yes, I'm dating myself). While I did not listen to many of his sermons,

I owned a John MacArthur study Bible with its copious notes. The Sunday school curriculum for my youth Sunday school class was R. C. Sproul's VHS series, "Dust to Glory." When I wasn't using my JMac study Bible, I read R. C. Sproul's *New Geneva Study Bible.* I listened to sermons constantly, albeit they were burned on CDs and carried around in a three-ring, zipper binder (again, admitting my age). I even took Shane & Shane songs and mashed them up with sermon clips. I was making my own sermon jams and sharing them with my like-minded friends. I say all this merely to explain my history as a student of all things related to conservative, Protestant theology. Maybe I was a "TheoBro" before the TheoBro term existed.

I fancied myself a defender of biblical truth. I created a now-defunct website titled "No Compromise Ministries," named in honor of my musical hero, Keith Green. It was a lot like a modern-day discernment blog in that it was a blog with little discernment. I warned everyone about everything. I considered myself to be fearless, which was easy when you are living with your parents and hiding behind a keyboard. No one was safe from *my* apologetics. I was a Gen X Martin Luther with the same stomach problems, more sobriety, and less profanity.

On one occasion, I vividly recall debating a young lady at a Christian concert. She told me, "I don't believe in the doctrine of election." Providentially for her, the concert was being held at a bookstore. So I walked to the Bible section, turned to Romans 9, pointed at the word *election*, and said, "Then you don't believe in the Bible." She cried. I laughed. As the kids today would say, I "owned" her, which is to say I won through a method of shaming. I didn't care if I was a jerk to my sister in Christ. It only mattered I was right.

Miraculously, I matured. Somewhat. I secured a great job in IT, got married, moved out of my parents' house, and bought my first home. I soon started seminary and began preparing for ministry.

As God blessed my wife and I with sons, I attempted to form them into what I perceived to be a sanctified vision of masculinity. I don't mention the theological influences, that I have to say, were responsible for my poor vision of masculinity. To the contrary, I mention MacArthur, Piper, and Sproul to say that while I thought I had my theology right, it didn't impact my life and parenting the way it should have. I should have known better. While I could recite the fruit of the Spirit, they were not very evident in my own life. I had a head knowledge that needed to be relocated to my heart. My boys had to be tough, but it wasn't the kind of toughness you found in God's Word. It was a worldly toughness. Tenderheartedness was for girls. Until it wasn't anymore. My idea of what it meant to be a man started to come apart beside that dugout in south Arkansas, but my reformation went into full-speed mode when I started thinking through how to disciple my children to follow Jesus.

For the entirety of my boys' young lives, I had been teaching them that men must keep their emotions in check. That was not in a healthy, "be self-controlled" kind of way but an apathetic, stoic way. They were not allowed to cry unless they were genuinely hurt. I taught them they needed to do well in school to get an excellent job with a good salary, find a wife, and raise a family. I taught them to throw the first punch if they were ever bullied. These were the things that would make them "real men." Yet there was Jesus, single and chaste His whole life, encouraging us to turn the other cheek while preaching good news to those oppressed by the powerful (Luke 4:18–19). He wept at his friend's funeral and described Himself as "gentle and lowly" (Matt. 11:29–30). He even applied motherly language to Himself, describing His desire for Jerusalem's repentance like a mother hen who longs to gather her chicks (Luke 13:34–35).[3]

Some respond to this description of Jesus by first demarcating between Christ's humiliation and His glorification. Humiliation refers to Christ's status during the incarnation, when He gave up certain elements of God's glory. Glorification is as it sounds: Christ's restoration of His glory upon His resurrection (John 17:3–5). A response, therefore, to the gentle and lowly Jesus is to say those attributes were true of His humiliation but not necessarily about His glorification. In other words, they argue against those characterizations of Jesus and their significance for our lives by insisting that the descriptions no longer apply because Jesus is no longer in a state of humiliation but rather glorification.

I do not completely disagree. Jesus is glorified now. Yet we are not. And the example Jesus left us to follow is not His glorified state but His life on the earth. Yes, we can and must anticipate the glorified state that awaits all His followers. This is the hope of glory disciples possess in Christ. Yet the hope of what is to come empowers us to persevere and endure in the now while we have the same mind of Christ (Phil. 2:5–11), which Paul takes to mean Christ's humility.

This is not to deny that God's kingdom has broken into the present world in such a way that those who are in Christ are not truly "a new creation" (2 Cor. 5:17). But it is to remind us that there is an undeniable "not yet" to our enjoyment in the new creation. If we are not careful, we will, as theologians describe it, "overrealize" our eschatology. Make no mistake, we will share in His glory and be made like Him as He is when He appears, but that time is not yet here (1 John 2:28–3:3). We look forward to that time, but we must remember that to be His disciples in this world means to take up a cross. It means to follow Him in humble service. It means patiently enduring evil. It means being known for our love. It means putting on compassion like a garment. It means leaving room for the vengeance that belongs to God, not us.

Here is where my breakthrough occurred. As I reflected on what I was teaching my sons, I realized I was instilling in them a vision of what it means to be a man who would eventually undermine their respect of and commitment to Jesus. Without realizing it, I was teaching them that Jesus wasn't a real man. Was He fully human? Sure. But was He an actual man? Well, that depended on how I defined what it means to be a man. If they brought the vision of masculinity I had taught them into their gospel readings, they would either misread or miss Jesus altogether because He just didn't fit the paradigm.

What my sons and I were experiencing was similar to many in the first century who maintained certain expectations about the Messiah. They knew He would descend from David, but their vision of what He would be was more of a warrior than a poet. He would throw off Rome and restore Israel. Yet, when Jesus did not fit their expectations, they quit listening, quit following, and eventually killed Him.

Make no mistake: Jesus is absolutely a warrior. It's just that His enemy and means of conquering that enemy are different than people imagined. In their minds, the Messiah would never be someone who could be conquered.

Such a Savior was a scandal and a stumbling block. There was no way the Messiah would be crucified.

Jesus corrects our imbalance of what it means to be a man. For some, this means Jesus needs to be seen more as a warrior than a poet. We need to see the Jesus who turned over tables in righteous anger because of injustice. We need to see the Jesus who confronted Pharisees with strong words for their misunderstanding and application of God's law. We need to see the Jesus who was not afraid to pronounce judgment over unrepentant cities. But for others, correcting the imbalance means Jesus needs to be seen more as a poet than a warrior. We need to see the emotional and relational life of the Son of Man who weeps, sings, serves, and eats with the lowly and the outcast. As Justin Bailey writes, "For though Jesus is not averse to flipping tables (John 2:13–17), his more common practice is to sit at them, asking penetrating questions."[4] If you don't believe me, just read the Gospel of Luke and note how often Jesus is either headed to a meal, at a meal, or leaving a meal.[5]

We need Jesus to rebalance our vision of what it means to be a man in this world, living according to God's will. We need Jesus to correct our overrealized vision of masculinity that longs for a crown without a cross. We must be reminded that Jesus told us if any person would come after Him, they must deny themselves and take up their cross.

When Poets Were Warriors

To illustrate this idea of a rebalanced vision of what it means to be a man, I have chosen the image of the poet-warrior. The most obvious example of the poet-warrior in Scripture comes from the life of David. As a poet, David composed songs on his harp. He wrote and sang of the beauty of the Lord. He danced undignified in the joy of the Lord. He expressed his affections for his God in ways that would likely make many men uncomfortable. Yet David was also a mighty warrior. His fingers could play a harp and also wield a sword. He was fearless in the face of opposition. He was a great leader of the people of God. David did not have to cease to be a poet in order to be a warrior. There was a balance to his life. So, why not write this book from the perspective of David's life?

For all the good that can be said about and drawn from David's life, Christian men are not called to imitate him or have his mind. In fact, there are things about his life that no man should emulate. Even at his best, King David was a shadow of the Messiah who was to come in Jesus Christ. But now that the substance of the shadow is here, it is better for us to consider Jesus, great David's greater Son. In Jesus, the balance of the poet and the warrior is perfectly seen. We see tenderness and toughness in appropriate expression. We see a man gentle and meek enough to welcome children but strong enough to bear a cross.

We see what a perfect man looks like. So, while we will consider what the whole of Christian Scripture says about being a man, we will do so through a lens that recognizes Jesus as the ultimate fulfillment of what a man ought to be in this world.

Two Caveats

I want to be clear about two things from the get-go. First, I consciously wrote this book for men. Men, you are the audience. While I am happy for women to read this book, my intended audience is Christian men. That means I have avoided some of the caveats and nuance I would include if writing for a broader audience. The temptation with a book like this is to write in such a way as to make it applicable for everyone because this book is filled with reflections on Scripture and Scripture is for everyone. Many of the passages we will review in the coming pages have relevant application and theological insight for men and women, but my purpose is to make the applications and insights geared toward men. While everyone is welcome to buy, read, share, and give this book to others, please be aware I have a specific audience in mind who needs to hear a specific message. If there are men in your life you love and care about, you will understand why I have narrowed my audience. Join me in praying that

God would use the truth of His Word to strengthen men through the message of this book.

Second, and most important, I intend to look at the life and teaching of Jesus as a model for a renewed vision of what it means to be a man. To do this, I draw broadly on resources of theologians who have written on the person of Christ, often titled "Christology." With that said, this book should not be construed to communicate that the significance of Christology is primarily about how we ought to live as Christians or, in particular, as Christian men. What do I mean by that? I mean that while Jesus's life and teaching provide us with a pattern of living, a moral example, that is not the sum of His life and work as Lord and Savior. Furthermore, while I highlight the example of Christ, I am not suggesting that His atoning work is merely a moral example. I believe and wholeheartedly confess that Jesus's work was one of penal substitutionary atonement. I love this doctrine! I could sing "In Christ Alone" and "Before the Throne of God Above" every day of my life until I see Him face-to-face and not get tired of these truths! So, while Jesus's life and teaching do provide us with a moral example, there is more to Jesus than providing us with a paradigm for living as Christians in the world. But there is not less.

As the hymn writer would put it, I believe with all my heart that the sinner's "hope is built on nothing less than

Jesus' blood and righteousness," and that we ought not "trust the sweetest frame but wholly lean on Jesus' name."[6] The danger with a book like this is to instrumentalize the life and teachings of Jesus in such a way that leads to a moralism that guts the gospel of its efficacious nature. We will not get to heaven or be born again by being better men. What we need more than anything in the world is the transformation of our sinful selves by the power of the gospel of Christ.

So, as you read this book, know that much of what you will find in these pages is "downstream" from the fountainhead of our salvation in Jesus Christ. Studying the person and work of Jesus as an example of what it means to be a Christian man depends first on having a life-changing encounter with Jesus as Lord and Savior. If all you gain from this book is a list of characteristics you can implement in your life, then I've failed. Jesus is more than an example of masculinity, though He is not less. I want you to walk away from this book not only with a greater understanding of what it means to be a man according to God's will but also with a greater love for Jesus Christ, who provides the greatest example of what it means to be a man while doing what only He could do: redeeming humanity from sin through His life, death, and resurrection.

Chapter 1

WHERE DO WE BEGIN?

If I'm being completely honest, it feels a little weird to write this chapter. I'm writing it while watching my oldest son play a high school baseball game. During a mid-inning break, I ran to the restroom so that I wouldn't miss any of the game. When walking up to the restrooms, I looked for the door labeled "Men." Next to the word *Men* was a symbol of what society has recognized as representing a man for ages. As I approached the door, I thought to myself, *Well, I know which door I am supposed to enter.* I did not suffer any sort of existential crisis. I knew which restroom door to enter because I inherently know that I am a man. I'm not confused about it. Neither are most men in society.

We know what it means to be a man from a biological perspective. We have XY chromosomes. We typically have higher levels of testosterone, more bone density, greater muscle mass, external sexual reproductive organs, and deeper voices. This is just the natural outworking of our genetic difference with women. God has fearfully and wonderfully made us as men. Men and women are different. And there is nothing evil or wrong about those differences. This is how God made us. To paraphrase theologian John Kleinig, we do not make our bodies; they were given to us and remain with us as the "foundation" for life here on the earth.[1] We should embrace the bodies God has given us. They are a gift from God and should be celebrated.

The physical differences between men and women are part of God's good creation. They are not the result of the fall of man. If we are going to understand anything about what it means to be a man, we must be clear on the givenness of our created bodies as men. We don't need to be embarrassed by this reality. Our differences are not bad.

But this is not a book about mere biological realities. Nor is this a book about the current language game being played in our society regarding issues like transgenderism.[2] I'm not going to argue for the recognition of the differences that are already clearly seen by those who have eyes to see them. Men and women are biologically different, and the differences are good, not because it's better to be one or the other but because God has made us "male and female," in His image (Gen. 1:27). So, if this book is not about mere biological realities, what is it about? This is a book about the theological realities that men are mandated by our Creator to reflect in the world as men. In other words, what does it mean to be a man as God intended?

What We Observe in God's Word

To frame our consideration of what it means to be a man as God intended, I want to start with an overview of what we observe in God's Word. This overview follows the grand story of the Bible from creation, to the fall of man, to the redemption we have in Christ. When I say *overview*, I've tried to provide a fast-paced and simplified look at key biblical themes related to our discussion about Jesus and manhood. It won't take long. But before I begin, I want to speak to the guys who might be inclined to put the book down at this point because they were looking for something immediately applicable to their life.

Men, the impulse to jump to the application without the theology is not good. Why? Because if we move to the *work* of our calling without understanding the *purpose* (or *telos*) of our calling, we risk the perversion of our work. We will get to the *work* of our calling in due time, but if you desire the most benefit from that work, you need to understand how it fits into the story God is telling in the world. So let's begin with creation.

Creation: Created Masculinity

If we are going to understand anything about what it means to be a man, let alone being a human, we must understand something of creation. Timothy Tennent says, "The central theology of the creation account is summarized in Genesis 5:1–2, *which says*, 'When God created mankind, he made them in the likeness of God. He created them male and female and blessed them. And he named them "mankind" when they were created.'"[3]

Furthermore, as another scholar puts it, "If we leave God's reality out of account, we cannot know whether we are real. But if we accept God's Word about that, we can know that we are. Conversely, that declaration affirms that the world does not exist in or of or for itself, independently of God, but only because God willed it."[4]

Creation establishes our entire existence in relationship to God's will. We know what we are and how we are to live because God has revealed and reinforced His will for us in Scripture. Let's begin with Genesis 2:5–7, which says,

> "When no bush of the field was yet in the land and no small plant of the field had yet sprung up—for the LORD God had not caused it to rain on the land, and there was no man to work the ground, and a mist was going up from the land and was watering

> the whole face of the ground—then the LORD God formed the man of dust from the ground and breathed into his nostrils the breath of life, and the man became a living creature."

There are a few things we can observe from this passage about what it means to be a man. First, we would not exist if God did not will for us to exist. We are not self-sufficient beings. Only God is self-sufficient. Humanity is not. As men we need God. He does not need us. Another way of stating this would be to say that we are stewards of our bodies and the rest of the created world, not owners.

While God does not need us, He, in His sovereign wisdom, chose to create us and employ us in His work. Note what the passage says: "The LORD God formed the man of dust from the ground and breathed into his nostrils the breath of life, and the man became a living creature." We are creatures formed of dust but filled with the breath of God to live and work in His creation. Thus, we observe that we possess life and purpose because God created us, which gets at what I mentioned earlier about the relationship between our work in the world and God's purpose for us. Have you ever felt like your work was meaningless? Like the things you do, day in and day out, are all done in vain? Part of the reason this is the case is because we have divorced our work in the world from God's purpose for us.

Much of the reason our work feels in vain is because we do not view ourselves as stewards but as owners. And tragically, when stewards begin to think they are owners, we end up being thieves. Instead of managing God's creation, we exploit it. Instead of marrying and rejoicing in the wife of our youth (Prov. 5:18–19), we end up being "half-hearted creatures, fooling around with drink and sex and ambition when infinite joy is offered us, like an ignorant child who wants to go on making mud pies in a slum because he cannot imagine what is meant by the offer of a holiday at the sea. We are far too easily pleased."[5] A proper understanding of creation and God's purpose for us as men in that creation can deliver us from the thievery of joy that happens when we think we own ourselves and the world we live in.

Men, we must grasp something of the weight and gravity of our creatureliness. John Calvin put it this way: "We cannot have a clear and complete knowledge of God unless it is accompanied by a corresponding knowledge of ourselves. This knowledge of ourselves is twofold: namely, to know what we were like when we were first created and what our condition became after the fall of Adam."[6] We will get to the fall of humanity shortly, but for now, we need to reflect on "what we were like when we were first created."

If we are creatures, then it follows that we are not the Creator. This distinction is crucial for living in humility before God and others. Again, Calvin makes a great point about the importance of remembering who we are as creatures. On Genesis 2:7, he wrote, "First we must realize that when he was taken from earth and clay [Gen. 2:7; 18:27], his pride was bridled. For nothing is more absurd than for those who not only 'dwell in houses of clay' [Job 4:19], but who are themselves in part earth and dust, to boast of their own excellence."[7]

Men, you are not God. Despite what the influencers on social media say, we are not self-made. We are creatures, not Creator. Any creative work you do is ultimately empowered by and a reflection of God's ultimate work in creation.

Men, it is so important for us to remember who we are. We are of dust, but we are also more than dust. We have a unique relationship to God as those who have received His breath.[8] While animals were created by God, humanity was created by God and filled by Him that we might become a "living being." So, while we need to be humble by remembering that we are dust, we also need to see the uniqueness of bearing God's image. What is an image? Again, Timothy Tennent is helpful: "An image is a reflection or representation of something else. . . . The biblical authors use the words *image* and *likeness* to convey that God endows humans with certain capacities that will enable them to "reflect" or "image" God in the world. . . . God created us to "image" or reflect something of His divine life."[9]

We are not animals. We are image bearers, vice-regents of the Lord God, tasked with the responsibility of extending His glory throughout all of creation.

Taken together, we can conclude with Gregory of Nyssa, who said, "In this world I have discovered the two affirmations that man is nothing and that man is great. If you consider nature alone, he is nothing and has no value; but if you regard the honor with which he has been treated, man is something great."[10]

This is a great starting place for us. Some of us need to be reminded that we are but dust. In and of ourselves, there are no naturally great men. This should humble us. However, when adequately humbled by seeing who we are before God, we can then begin to walk in the honor God has bestowed on us.

This means that because of your relationship to God, you don't have to prove your worth in this world. You don't have to prove your manliness in the world because you are as God created you. Your manliness doesn't depend on how much you can bench press, how many deer you have harvested, how many women you have slept with, how much money you earn, or how much others admire you. I love how one theologian described this aspect of creation.

He said, "That a male human is manly simply by being male, and that this is good, seems obvious. Yet it is often not accepted as a given, a good gift which a man should be glad to receive and live out. Many men have an apparent need to achieve being manly, to 'prove' that they are men, typically expressed in a conquest approach to male sexuality."[11]

In other words, when we fail to see ourselves as God has created us in relationship to Him and the rest of His creation, things start to go poorly, which is what we see in the chapters of Genesis that follow the account of creation.

Fall: Broken Masculinity

While God declares His creation of man and woman to be "very good" and subsequently unites the two together in marriage, it does not take long for things to go bad. Theologians call this the "fall of man," which refers to Adam and Eve's rebellion against God and their expulsion from the garden of Eden and God's presence. I won't rehearse all of the details of this account in great depth here, but there are some important things that we need to see for the sake of our study of biblical masculinity.

First, we see Adam and Eve given to each other in marriage. They have a responsibility to subdue the earth and fill it with offspring. They are given one prohibition: do not eat of the fruit of the tree of the knowledge of good and evil. Shortly after receiving this prohibition, a serpent, later identified in Scripture as Satan, deceives Eve to eat the forbidden fruit in the presence of Adam. There is no indication that Adam was not there. Instead of obeying God, Adam and Eve questioned what the Lord had told them. Eve ate the fruit and then gave it to her husband Adam, who also ate of it. Immediately their eyes were opened to their nakedness. They hid in shame from each other and from the Lord. Yet the Lord came to them in the garden, and while faithful to His promise to curse them with death if they ate of the forbidden fruit, He also clothed them with animal skins and cursed the serpent who had deceived them.

The result of this fall into sin in the garden of Eden would be that man's labor on the earth would get substantially harder. Note that the passage does not say Adam would have to start working, as if work itself were a result of the fall. No, work itself is good. Yet work in a fallen world would be harder than previously imagined. For Eve, her labor in rearing children would be harder. Because of sin, Adam and Eve's relationship would become more difficult. Desires of the flesh would rule over them, making the bliss of marriage something harder to maintain. Finally, the couple would be removed from the garden of Eden to sojourn in the wild country until a day would come when the Seed of the woman would finally crush the head of the serpent and free them from their bondage to sin and death. Even in the sadness of their rebellion, God gave them hope that things would not always be as broken as they currently were. At this point, we could spend a lot of time detailing the way sin impacted the whole world, but we are focusing on how sin impacted men and their view of masculinity. So I want focus on how the fall of man is reflected in the broken masculinity we see in Scripture.

One of the first glimpses we get of broken masculinity is in Genesis 4 with the account of two brothers, Cain and Abel, born to Adam and Eve. Cain was the oldest son. In fact, some commentators note that Eve's words, which are recorded in Genesis 4:1, indicate that she may have thought this child would be the Seed who would deliver them from the curse. Tragically, the son she thought might be her deliverer would actually compound her grief. Cain worked the ground, and Abel worked with the sheep. When it was time to offer a sacrifice to the Lord, Abel's sacrifice was accepted while Cain's was rejected. Cain was outraged with the Lord and decided to exact revenge on Abel. Cain murdered his own brother because of his jealousy. Here in Cain we see an example of broken masculinity. Instead of using the strength God had given him to obey the Lord, he used his strength to commit fratricide.

As a result of Cain's sin, he, much like his father Adam, was cursed and banished from the land. To be sure, the Lord swore to protect him. He did not end Cain's life immediately, but Cain's life was filled with sorrow. Cain moved, married, and was blessed with a son. Cain built a city for his growing family. And eventually, he had a descendent named Lamech, who is a tragic example of broken masculinity.

Lamech is the first person in the Bible who is described as taking more than one wife. This is significant since the creation order revealed that a man should marry one woman and build a family with her alone. Lamech, however, is given to excess. He marries two women instead of one. Furthermore, Lamech is a violent man. In Genesis 4:23–24, we read the record of Lamech's song of excess. He brags that he has two wives, then glories in his disproportionate response to being wronged by others. He kills those who merely wound him. And he sings about it! Lamech glorifies his godlessness.

When I read about Lamech, I cannot help but see parallels between what some in our day consider the marks of a "real man." Here is Lamech, a man wealthy enough to take two wives for himself and a man who shows no restraint in his responses to those who harm him. Lamech knows this is not honoring to God. He basically confesses this when he says if "Cain's revenge is sevenfold, then Lamech's is seventy-sevenfold" (Gen. 4:24). Lamech is a broken man who thinks his gratuitous lust and violence are things to admire. To paraphrase what one scholar said of Lamech, "He is a self-secure man,"[12] or at least he thinks he is.

Men, we were not made to be like Lamech, yet I see so many of us looking to "influencers" who basically live a life much like Lamech's. Maybe a good test for how we're doing in terms of judging our masculinity would be found by asking ourselves, "Whom do I admire more—Abel or Cain and Lamech?" Do I regard Abel as weak because he was a victim of his brother's violence? Or do I regard him as the author of Hebrews did, "righteous . . . and through his faith, though he died, he still speaks" (Heb. 11:4)? Let this comparison confront the disposition of your heart.

We could follow this kind of pattern throughout Scripture, and I'll do my best to point it out as we encounter it. For now, I want you to see how sin has this tendency to take the good things about man and turn them for evil. Strength is not bad. God made men to be strong. Yet we must remember why He gave us the strength. It was not to exact disproportionate violence on those who wrong us. Furthermore, as God blessed us with the ability to earn income and build wealth, He did so that we might be generous toward others, blessing them as God has blessed us. He did not bless us that we might make a name for ourselves but that His name might be great. What needs to happen for men to use their gifts as God intended them?

We need the transforming grace of God, which we begin to see more clearly in the redemption that unfolds next.

Redemption: Redeemed Masculinity

While the world was moving from bad to worse (Gen. 6:5–7), one man found favor in the eyes of the Lord (Gen. 6:8). Through the obedience of Noah, a people would be carried safely through the judgment waters of the flood. Once the ark found a resting place, Noah and his family were given a mandate similar to the one given to Adam and Eve. They were to be fruitful and multiply, filling the earth again (Gen. 9:7). Noah's family would do just this, though not without some major dysfunction (Gen. 10–11).

At the end of Genesis 11, we are introduced to an important man named Abram, who would eventually be called Abraham. God called Abraham and promised to make his name great as the father of a great nation (Gen. 12:1–3). But there was a problem. Abraham and his wife Sarah (Sarai) were old, past childbearing age. If the promise was going to be fulfilled, then God would have to do it miraculously. And, of course, God did. Despite Sarah and Abraham's reliance first on the flesh—their own plan apart from God (Gen. 16; cf. Gal. 4:21–31)—God allowed Sarah to conceive and bear a son named Isaac, the son of promise. His existence depended on the work of God in Abraham and Sarah's life.

The giving of Isaac clues us into the fact that God is the God who works in seemingly impossible circumstances. Such a God demands our faith. And, as the story unfolds, God fulfills the promise that He called Abraham to embrace by faith. By this faith Abraham was justified—that is, declared righteous before God (Rom. 4:1–5:11; Gal. 3:1–29). By trusting God instead of relying on the flesh, Abraham had Isaac. Then Isaac had Jacob. Jacob's name would eventually be changed to Israel, and he would have twelve sons. The descendants of those twelve sons would eventually become the people of Israel.

In keeping with the promise God made Abraham, Israel was to become a blessing to all the nations of the earth (Gen. 12:2). These descendants would multiply and mature into a nation who would eventually ask the prophet Samuel to anoint a king for them so they could be like the other nations (1 Sam. 8). In spite of the prophet's warnings, rooted in the Lord's rebuke of His people for wanting a king other than Him, Israel got what it wanted. And his name was Saul.

First Samuel 9:2 describes Saul as "a handsome young man. There was not a man among the people of Israel more handsome than he. From his shoulders upward he was taller than any of the people." In other words, Saul was a man's man. Handsome, young, tall, and powerful. The kind of guy a pastor search committee is hoping they will find to lead their church. The type of guy who just looks like a leader from central casting. Yet Saul, while a man, was not a good man.

Saul was rebellious, violating the commands of the Lord regarding sacrifices (1 Sam. 13:8–23). He made rash decisions that jeopardized the well-being of others (1 Sam. 14:24–46). And he was man of what I would call "selective" use of force. Sure, he could lead an army into battle, but when the confrontation called for the possibility of personal loss, he was a coward (1 Sam. 17). Israel needed a new king; someone who would obey the Lord.

When the Lord called Samuel to anoint another king to replace Saul, He explicitly told him that when looking for the one the Lord had chosen, "Do not look on his appearance or on the height of his stature, . . . for the LORD sees not as man sees: man looks on the outward appearance, but the LORD looks on the heart" (1 Sam. 16:7). This was in response to Samuel's initial enthusiasm at finding a man who was much like Saul in appearance. But God would accomplish His purposes in a manner that would confound the wisdom of man once again.

Enter David, a lyre-playing poet-shepherd who was a somewhat forgotten son of a man named Jesse. Jesse had not thought to invite his youngest son to the king-making party. He was busy with the sheep, fighting off threats to the family's livelihood, and probably passing the time with his instrument. While Scripture describes David as having "beautiful eyes" and being "handsome" (1 Sam. 16:12), these were not his most important qualities. David feared God. Oswald Chambers puts it this way: "The remarkable thing about God is that when you fear God, you fear nothing else, whereas if you do not fear God, you fear everything else."[13] Nowhere was this fearlessness on display more than on the battlefield with Goliath (1 Sam. 17). While Saul and the other Israelites feared Goliath, David feared God. Thus, the lyre-playing poet-shepherd struck down Goliath, the giant warrior.

In time, David became the king of Judah then Israel, uniting the twelve tribes under his leadership. Of course, this journey to the kingship was not without its obstacles. For one, Saul was threatened by David, which led him to try to kill the young man on multiple occasions. The Lord, however, protected David. Saul was eventually killed in battle, and David was officially made king. But we would be remiss not to mention David's failures as well. David took multiple wives (1 Sam. 30) and stole another man's wife while conspiring to have that man killed in the process (2 Sam. 11). While David was a good king, he was not a perfect man. He embodied many admirable characteristics, yet he was a complex character in the story God was telling. David would rule over Israel, but he would struggle to manage his dysfunctional household. If the nation of people created from Abraham's lineage was to get the king they needed, God Himself would have to intervene.

In 2 Samuel 7:1–17, the Lord promised David, much as He had promised Abraham, that He would "make for you a great name, like the name of the great ones of the earth" (v. 9). But while David and many of His descendants like Solomon did some good, they could not change the hearts of the people. Thus, we see that the fulfillment of 2 Samuel 7:1–17 would have to come from above. God Himself would come to turn His people's hearts to Him, which is exactly what we see in Jesus Christ, the Son of David, the Son of Abraham, God with us (Matt. 1:1, 23).

The one man who could undo the devastation brought about by the first Adam would be Jesus, the last Adam (1 Cor. 15:45). The one man who could ultimately build a great nation of renown was not one of the multiple descendants of Abraham but Jesus, the Seed of Abraham (Gal. 3:16). The one Man who could ultimately rule over God's people was not Solomon or Josiah or any other number of David's immediate relatives but Jesus the Christ, great David's greater son (Mark 12:35–37). By taking on flesh and dwelling among us (John 1:14), Jesus makes God known (John 1:18) and fulfills all that He had promised for His people (2 Cor. 1:20). But as Jesus makes God known to us, He also shows us how to live. As such, Jesus is the perfect man, and if we would learn anything about what it means to be a man, we need to be transformed by His grace, being given eyes to see and ears to hear that we might be saved and conformed to His image (Rom. 8:29).

This book is all about looking to Jesus for our answer to the question, What does it mean to be a man? In Jesus, we find the perfect balance of an authentic, sinless life before God and before others. We see a perfect example to follow in our pursuit of living as the men God created us to be in the world.

Conclusion

Our most desperate need is to be transformed by God's grace in Jesus Christ through the Holy Spirit. More than sex, violence, or power, if you want to be the kind of man God intends for you to be, then your old self must be put to death (Eph. 4:22–24). You need to become a new creation in Christ (2 Cor. 5:17). No degree of habit stacking, gym routines, supplements, biohacking, education, YouTube seminars, or Joe Rogan podcasts will make you the kind of man God desires you to be. While those things may have some value, ultimately we are changed through godliness by faith in Jesus Christ. His work in us creates contentment in our hearts (1 Tim. 4:7–8).

Men, the issue with our masculinity is not that it is too deep but that it's too shallow. Our vision of masculinity is too superficial. To be sure, we are men simply because God created us as men. Yet there is also a nurturing and nourishing of our manliness as God intended it, which should be in keeping with what we see in Jesus Christ, the perfect man. So maybe we ought to reframe our initial question. Maybe it's misguided to ask, "What does it mean to be a man?" Instead, maybe we should be asking, "What does it mean to be the type of man God has revealed in Jesus Christ?"

In the chapters that follow, my hope is to expose us to Jesus's example and teaching on vital issues that impact us as men. My prayer is that it would be profitable for our growth as men created for God's glory and the good of others.

Chapter 2

THE EMOTIONAL LIFE OF GODLY MEN

If someone were to describe you as "emotional," would you regard it as a compliment or an insult? Think about it for a moment. How we respond to that question tells us a lot about how we are conditioned to think about human emotions. If your response to such a description causes you to protest, "I'm not emotional!," it's probably because you've been taught that there is something inherently weak to being perceived as emotional. Jason Wilson writes, "From childhood through early puberty then into manhood, we're conditioned to swallow our pain, expressing little but indifference and detachment about the chaos around us."[1] Deep down we know there is something wrong with this kind of emotional suppression. What human is not, in truth, an emotional being? We are not machines. What a sad existence to believe that expressing our God-given emotions makes us less of a man.

Some of our problem stems from the inclination of men to avoid being described in a manner in which women are typically described. Where emotional expression among women is regarded as normal, men are told, "No emotion for you!" Men, I get it. We are men and therefore different from women, which includes how we express our emotions. There is nothing necessarily wrong with maintaining a differentiation in the expression of emotions. Our embodiment as male creatures bestows on us some differences whether we like it or not. Yet, in our efforts to maintain differentiation—say, asserting women as emotional creatures and men as nonemotional creatures, we have gone too far and cut ourselves off from our humanity. This is one of the many reasons we must look to Jesus as we sort through our questions about masculinity. As men, we should desire to live fully human lives that God has gifted us with for His glory and the good of others. That includes the fact that we do have a range of emotions. So, what does it look like for a man to be fully human as a man?

The Emotional Life of Our Lord

B. B. Warfield began his great essay titled, "On the Emotional Life of Our Lord," with the following sentence: "It belongs to the truth of our Lord's humanity, that he was subject to all sinless human emotions.[2] Warfield admits that this may be hard for us to fathom since our own experience with human emotion is tainted by sin. Nevertheless, if we refuse to wrestle with Christ's perfect humanity, emotions included, we risk misunderstanding what it means to be fully human as men.

So, what did the emotional life of Jesus look like? Stephen Wellum provides a great starting point for us in his book, *God the Son Incarnate: The Doctrine of Christ.* Wellum summarizes the "full range of human emotions, needs, and characteristics" exhibited by Jesus. He writes,

> He was moved to pity, compassion, love, and affection (Matt. 9:36; Mark 1:41; 8:2; Luke 7:36–50; John 11:5; 13:34; 15:9–13); he was distressed (Mark 7:34; 8:12; Luke 22:15, 44); he became angry (Mark 3:5; John 11:33, 38); he experienced joy (Luke 10:21; John 15:11); he got annoyed (Mark 10:14); he was surprised (Matt. 8:10; Mark 6:6) and disappointed (Mark 8:17; 9:19); he remained subject to his parents (Luke 2:51); he suffered hunger and thirst (Matt. 4:1–2; Mark 11:12; John 19:28), fatigue and weariness (Matt. 8:23–24; John 4:5–6), and temptation (Luke 4:2, 13; 22:28), and he offered up prayers with loud cries and tears (Matt. 26:36–46; cf. Heb. 5:7).[3]

If Jesus, in His perfect humanity, experienced such emotions, needs, and characteristics, why do we feel like some of these things are off-limits to us? Do we think we are better men than Jesus? Are we too proud to have pity on others? Too firm to show compassion? Too cold to show love and affection? Too strong to ever be distressed? Too apathetic to ever get angry? Too depressed to ever experience real joy? Too isolated to ever get annoyed? Too aloof to be surprised? Too hopeless to be disappointed? Too lazy to become weary? Too passive to fight temptation? Too timid to ever raise our voice in prayers to God before others? Too embarrassed to weep with those who weep or mourn with those who mourn? Again, I ask, Are we better men than Jesus? Obviously, the answer to that last question is "Not on your life!" No one was a better man than Jesus, yet His true and sinless masculinity did not prevent Him from living a fully human life that included emotions.

For some of us, this example found in Jesus ought to awaken our emotions. This means that some of us need to learn to have pity and compassion, even if you never saw it modeled in your fathers or grandfathers. Some of us need to put our phones away and hug our sons and our daughters, kiss our wives, and laugh a little bit in their presence. Some of us need to get off our tails and sweat a little bit around the house and in the yard or while wrestling or playing catch with our kids instead of just in the gym. We might need to raise our expectations enough to experience some disappointment instead of being cold and cynical. And at the same time, some of us don't need to apologize every time we get righteously angry or annoyed.

To be sure, there can be excesses in all these things, but don't let the fear of excess keep you from being real and expressive. Be a Christlike man in your expressiveness. We are aiming for the kind of emotional balance we see in Jesus. We'll fall short of His balance, of course, and that's okay. But we must be reminded we are not brutes or animals without self-control. Our purpose in the world (remember, *telos*) depends on a communion with God that works within us a disciplined life of temperance and self-control. Sometimes when I read others on the topic of masculinity, I wonder if they have considered how the demonic man's encounter with Jesus left him "sitting there, clothed and in his right man" (Mark 5:15). We are not beasts, brothers. We were made in the image of God, and though sin has warped us, in Christ by the Holy Spirit, we are a new creation (2 Cor. 5:17). We don't need to manufacture an adventure or cosplay our masculinity to feel like "real" men. We need to follow Christ, which will lead to a maturity that will do more good than machismo ever will.

Now, can there be excess in emotion? Yes. We should be mindful of our own sinfulness and how that sinfulness influences our emotions. Jesus expressed His emotions sinlessly. While we want to imitate Jesus, we need to remember that we are not Jesus. There is a tension here, and that's okay. Let's talk about two supposed ends of an emotional spectrum: anger and compassion.

Let's begin with the emotion of anger. You, as a man who has trusted in Christ, can and should express anger at times. How could we not express anger at the unrighteousness we see in our lives and the world around us? Anger *can* be a right and proper response. However, it is not the only response. Nor is it a response that is untethered from other good and godly emotions like love and compassion. It is also tethered to biblical obligations and expectations like the fruit of the spirit (Gal. 5:22–23). It is possible to be angry and loving all at once. This is one of the reasons Scripture tells us to "be angry and do not sin" (Eph. 4:26). Paul recognizes we're prone to expressing anger through sin; hence his command to "not sin." We must wrestle with the reality that we have emotions coupled with our sinful inclinations. Yet we should not allow the possibility of falling short in our emotions to keep us from showing our emotions.

There is a balance we must seek to maintain here that utterly depends on the work of the Holy Spirit conforming us to the image of God's Son, Jesus Christ. I appreciate what Benjamin Merkle had to say about Ephesians 4:26 regarding the command to "be angry": "Paul does not mean that Christians should be characterized by anger, but that they should appropriately express anger on certain occasions. That all anger is not sinful is demonstrated by the life of Jesus, who at times was angry (Mark 3:5) and yet was without sin (Heb. 4:15)."[4]

John Stott also gets it right: "There is a great need in the contemporary world for more Christian anger. . . . In the face of blatant evil we should be indignant not tolerant, angry not apathetic. If God hates sin, his people should hate it too. If evil arouses his anger, it should arouse ours also."[5]

Men, do you believe this? Or have you bought into the lie that tells you all forms of anger are inherently sinful and that you should just sit by with your mouth shut while our society sins from bad to worse lest you be accused of expressing "toxic masculinity"? Some of you need to consider how God is calling you to "be angry" in the spirit of Ephesians 4:26.

But what about compassion? Is it possible to be too compassionate? All of this depends on how we define *compassion*. If what we mean by compassion is something like being endlessly open, inviting, and tolerant of all peoples and practices, then yes, it's possible to be too compassionate. Why? Because such an understanding of compassion does harm, which in turn, means it isn't compassionate at all. If I, as a father, let my children play in a busy road because I want them to regard me as a "gentle" father who never hurts their feelings and lets them do whatever they desire, then I'm neither compassionate nor loving toward them. In fact, I'm apathetic to their well-being. It's not loving and compassionate to let others perish.

There is also a need for us to see that hard words of denunciation from Jesus in Matthew 11:20–24 were followed by the inviting words of salvation in verses 25–30. We need to balance our view of Jesus's strong words against Chorazin, Bethsaida, and Capernaum with the equally strong invitation to come to the Savior who describes Himself as "gentle and lowly" (v. 29). Likewise, the compassionate words of Matthew 11:25–30 need not ever mean that there is no place to pronounce woes in sinful rebellion. Jesus won't let us pigeonhole Him emotionally. The same Christ who got angry also wept. This Christ is worthy of our worship and imitation as men.

The Danger of Apathy

In its most basic form, the word *apathy* is used to convey the idea of being passionless. It comes from the Greek word *pathos*, which could refer, depending on the context, to some sort of suffering being endured (like Christ's sacrifice) or to an experience of a strong desire."[6] When you add the alpha privative before the word (a + pathy), you negate what follows. So apathy refers to a lack of feeling or the lack of emotion or strong desires. So, to speak of the danger of apathy, I'm talking about the danger of a lack of desire or emotion. This, I believe, is one of the hallmarks of a truly toxic masculinity.

Nothing threatens your heart and home quite like emotional indifference. Let me see if I can explain why this is so dangerous. One reason we see a growing cottage industry of material on masculinity—representing some of the worst of the worst views available—is because good men do little to nothing to confront it. Instead of being righteously angry and denouncing so much of what masquerades as masculinity, many men sit by claiming that there is a proverbial lion is the streets, so they better stay home and be safe (Prov. 22:13).

If we, as men, would follow Christ, we must be directed by Him. As Paul told the church in Philippi,

> "Have this mind among yourselves, which is yours in Christ Jesus, who, though he was in the form of God, did not count equality with God a thing to be grasped, but emptied himself, by taking the form of a servant, being born in the likeness of men. And being found in human form, he humbled himself by becoming obedient to

> the point of death, even death on a cross."
> (Phil. 2:5–8)

Humble, obedient, service, to the point of death. That is the mind we are to have. This is what we see in Jesus.

And in sacrifice, there will be tears and sweat and cries and surprises and disappointments and laughter and sadness. John Newton tells us, "Through many toils and snares."[7] But men, it's worth it! To us it has been granted to "not only believe in him but also suffer for his sake" (Phil. 1:29). Just as Jesus fulfilled His work on the earth while exhibiting the full range of human emotions, you too should expect to have a similar experience. It will not be an apathetic, passionless life. It will be full of passion, sanctified, holy, Christlike emotions that do not control us but rather aid us in our work to serve Christ, our families, our communities, and our world.

Conclusion

This is why I favor the image of "the poet as warrior" and "the warrior as poet" when thinking about retrieving a biblical vision of what it means to be a man. This is why we have to keep our focus on Christ during this retrieval. We need to see that being a man is not all poet, nor is it all warrior. The poet provides the emotional health the warrior needs to fulfill his purpose in the world. The warrior reminds the poet that the battle is real and eternity is at stake. The poet composes on the battlefield of life, reflecting on the work of the warrior empowered "not by might, nor by power, but by my Spirit" (Zech. 4:6).

Christ embodies this balance perfectly, beckoning us to deny ourselves, take up our cross, and follow Him (Mark 8:34). He reminds us that our warfare is not a matter of flesh and blood but of waging a spiritual war against our flesh and those principalities that long to destroy us and those we love. We find this example in Christ Himself, who, while waging the battle for the souls of mankind during the crucifixion, cried out in a loud voice, declaring Psalm 22, "My God, my God, why have you forsaken me?" (v. 1). Jesus was no apathetic man. He was a fully human man, marked by self-control, freely exhibiting sinless emotion, for God's glory and our good (Heb. 4:15). And men, he beckons us to follow Him as fully human men as well, emotions included.

Chapter 3

WEAKNESS IS THE WAY

Men, we are not doing well. In the West, men are disproportionately impacted by what some have labeled "diseases of despair." What is that? The phrase "diseases of despair" refers to mortality or morbidity resulting from "suicidality, drug abuse, and alcoholism."[1] In other words, most of these "diseases" are self-inflicted coping responses to some sort of difficulty or distress in a man's life or community. Men are increasingly turning to drugs, alcohol, and even suicide as a solution to the despair that they feel. In a world that possesses ever increasing health care and technology advances, the life expectancy of men continues to drop, and experts believe this is due in no small part to these self-inflicted attempts to cope with things like financial trouble, depression, and stress.

Men, we must realize that being a man does not mean we must suffer in silence. Instead, we have biblical examples in poetic language to lament, grieve, and cry out to God for strength. We do not have to fear appearing weak.

Why? Because, according to Scripture, we are weak, but our God is not. My hope is that this chapter will fill you with hope to cry out to God in your sense of weakness and find that He alone is our strength.

The Strength of Weakness

In 2 Corinthians, the apostle Paul was dealing with the claims of "super apostles" who had infiltrated the church in Corinth. From what we can tell, they were boasting about their spiritual strength, bragging about the fruitfulness of their ministry. As a result, the church in Corinth and likely some of the so-called "super apostles" themselves were calling Paul's apostolic ministry into question. You can imagine the people saying something like, "Look at how weak Paul is," or "Look at how Paul has been beaten and imprisoned. God must not be blessing his ministry." In their view, Paul seemed weak and ineffective. What would Paul do? Would he defend himself by saying, "Of course I'm not weak! Look at the strength of my ministry!"

How would you respond? Would you defend yourself with all your accomplishments? Would you brag about how many people you have discipled or how many churches you have planted? I mean, who wants to be perceived as weak? Despite the way we are inclined to respond in our flesh, Paul takes a different approach. In 2 Corinthians 12:9, Paul recounts a revelation he had received from Christ amid all his trials. He writes, "But he [that's Jesus] said to me, 'My grace is sufficient for you, for my power is made perfect in weakness.'" Do you catch that? Jesus had a purpose in Paul's weakness, which was to perfect His power in Paul. Perfecting Jesus's power in Paul is the idea of bringing His power to its fullness, or completion. In other words, if Paul wanted to know the fullness of Jesus's power, he would need to lean into his weakness instead of denying it.

Paul goes on to explain, "Therefore I will boast all the more gladly of my weaknesses, so that the power of Christ may rest upon me. For the sake of Christ, then, I am content with weaknesses, insults, hardships, persecutions, and calamities" (vv. 9–10). Wow. Boasting in my weakness! What a radical proposition. Paul realized that the power of Christ would rest on him in his weakness, not his strength. If that meant insults, hardships, persecution, or calamities, Paul knew it was better to be weak than strong. Why? So that only Christ would get the glory for what God accomplished through Paul.

Let me ask you, *Would you rather be strong in and of yourself and lack the power of Christ or be weak and have the power of Christ rest on you?* Be honest. I know what my flesh desires, and I bet I know what your flesh desires too. We want people in our churches and in our communities to admire us for our strength. We want to be admired, celebrated, and glorified for our own greatness. Think about the way people often bandy about Philippians 4:13 as some sort of promise of success. Everyone wants to quote, "I can do all things through [Christ] who strengthens me." But most people who quote it don't understand its context. They want that passage to mean they will always hit the walk-off home run to win the game or score the game-winning touchdown or make the presentation that seals the deal for the company. *Yes!*, they think, *I can do all these things through Christ who strengthens me.* But hardly anyone wants to point out that Paul wrote that while in prison. No one wants to think about the possibility that maybe that passage is more about being strengthened in weakness than looking successful in the eyes of others. Maybe it's about being strengthened by Christ when you are perceived as a failure.

All of this makes me think of one of my favorite golfers, Scottie Scheffler. As he entered the 2024 Masters tournament, he was asked about how his life would change if he won that week. He responded by essentially saying that while golf is obviously a big part of his life, it was not the essence of his identity. His identity was secure in Christ. So, whether he won or lost the tournament, who he is in Christ is secure. This reality strengthened him. What a relief to know that whether you win or lose, or as Paul would say in Philippians 4, where he abounds or is demeaned, Christ is your strength, the hope of your life forever. This gets at the real heart of what Paul is saying in Philippians 4:13, and it also helps us make sense of 2 Corinthians 12:9–10.

As Paul concludes his thought at the end of verse 10, he states, “For when I am weak, then I am strong.” This seems like such a contradiction. Our inclination is to respond and say, “No, Paul. You are either weak or strong. You can’t be both.” But Paul won’t play by our rules. He is saying that his real strength comes from the Lord (Ps. 121:1–2). He doesn’t look to himself for strength but to God. And as I have thought about the strongest men I’ve ever known, it is consistently proven true that they are the kind of men who recognize their weakness and need for God. As a result, they know an unshakable strength. They are willing not to be the hero in their story so the power of Christ might be made perfect in them. We need to see that the way of weakness really is the way of strength.

What are we to do, however, when we are so acutely aware of our weakness that we are paralyzed with fear and despair? This is where we must strike a balance lest we fall prey to those “diseases of despair” I mentioned earlier. It is one thing to be reminded of our identity and strength in Christ. This is crucial. But we also need to be reminded of the resources this identity and strength bring to bear on our lives in the moments when the darkness of life won't lift.

Pushing Back the Darkness

Years ago, I preached a sermon on Psalm 88 that did not get the response I had hoped from the congregation. It was the first sermon in a series titled "Battling Depression." If you are at all familiar with Psalm 88, you probably know that it is a dark psalm. It's not really a "Christmas card letter" or "wedding invitation" kind of passage. I began the sermon with a series of comments from Edward T. Welch's book on depression.[2] Think about how you feel when you hear these descriptions.

> Hell came to pay me a visit. A lonely, private hell. I feel as though I died a few weeks ago and my body hasn't found out yet. My bones waste away, my groaning all day long. That is all I want in life: for this pain to seem purposeful. There was not control on my mind—thoughts ravaged me, brutally harsh ideas, thoroughly crush ideals, incomprehensible feelings. You don't feel as though you know much. The only thing you know is that you are guilty, shameful, and worthless. It is not

> that you have made mistakes in your life or sinned or reaped futility. It is that you are a mistake; you are sin; you are futility. You are confident that everyone would be better off without you.[3]

Dark stuff, right? While these descriptions are dark, they are often true to life and consistent with the kind of things we see in Scripture. Consider how Psalm 88 ends. After the psalmist recounts his anguish before the Lord, he concludes the psalm with these words: "You have distanced loved one and neighbor from me; darkness is my only friend" (v. 18 CSB). Yes, that's where the psalm *ends*.

After service, I typically stood at the back door to greet members as they left for lunch. One church member pulled me aside after that sermon and told me something like, "I hope you never preach a sermon like that again." Funny, when you preach on battling depression, you don't hope to experience a taste of it on account of church member feedback. Nevertheless, while that particular church member didn't appreciate the message, many did because they felt seen. Many were suffering emotionally, and the language of lament and grief captured in Psalm 88 allowed their desperate hearts to know that God can handle any of their emotions.

I want you to notice two things in Psalm 88. First, the psalmist is willing to beg the Lord to hear him. He's desperate. Have you ever felt desperate? If so, you are in good company, and God, in His mercy, is not repulsed by our desperate cries to be heard. The second thing is that after begging the Lord to hear him, the psalmist entrusts his cries to the Lord. In fact, that is what the majority of the psalm is: entrusting complaints to the Lord who alone can remedy the man's situation.

As men, we've got to learn the language of lament with hope, which we see in Psalm 88. Too many of us are suffering in silence and isolation due to dark feelings. Some of us are scared to name those dark feelings. Maybe we feel like labeling it "depression" is too feminine. Many of us, after all, were taught we should hide our feelings. But contrary to what you may think, you're never good at hiding your feelings. Your feelings will find a way out. It might not always look like what others think is depression, but the violent outbursts, the substance addictions, or the compulsive behaviors that seek to quell the longing in our souls are indicators that something is not right in our life. When we feel like Psalm 88, we need to learn to pray like Psalm 88. Men, we need to be reverently and fearfully honest with God about the things we are feeling. We don't need to turn to drinks or drugs or some other vice to sedate these feelings. We need to turn to God, just as we see Jesus do in His moment of great distress.

Go to Dark Gethsemane

When Jesus faced the prospect of death under God's justice, at the hands of unrighteous people (Acts 2; 4), He entrusted Himself to God (1 Pet. 2). He did not seek to dull the pain, though He understandably and righteously pleaded. Consider Matthew 26:36–46, which reads,

> Then Jesus went with them to a place called Gethsemane, and he said to his disciples, "Sit here, while I go over there and pray." And taking with him Peter and the two sons of Zebedee, he began to be sorrowful and troubled. Then he said to them, "My soul is very sorrowful, even to death; remain here, and watch with me." And going a little farther he fell on his face and prayed, saying, "My Father, if it be possible, let this cup pass from me; nevertheless, not as I will, but as you will." And he came to the disciples and found them sleeping. And he said to Peter, "So, could you not watch with me one hour? Watch and pray that you may not enter into temptation. The spirit indeed is willing, but the flesh is weak." Again, for the second time, he went away and prayed, "My Father, if

> this cannot pass unless I drink it, your will be done." And again he came and found them sleeping, for their eyes were heavy. So, leaving them again, he went away and prayed for the third time, saying the same words again. Then he came to the disciples and said to them, "Sleep and take your rest later on. See, the hour is at hand, and the Son of Man is betrayed into the hands of sinners. Rise, let us be going; see, my betrayer is at hand."

In this passage, we see Jesus described as "sorrowful and troubled," but before we consider what this description means, we need to see that just prior to His time in the garden of Gethsemane, Jesus is singing praises to God with His disciples (Matt. 26:30). Given the proximity of this scene to the Passover and the relationship of the Lord's Supper, which Jesus had just instituted for His disciples, it is fair to assume that Jesus and the disciples had just finished singing a hymn of praise to God. It may be that hymn was taken from passages like Psalms 116:8–14; 117; or 118:5–7, 26–29. These hymns of praise to God express confidence in God's victory over His enemies. They extol His power and faithfulness. So, just moments before Jesus is fighting the battle for the souls of His people in the garden of Gethsemane, He is singing poetic verses of praise to God.

Admittedly, I find the lyrics of some contemporary Christian songs to be corny and shallow. There's one song in particular that refers to a melody functioning like a weapon. Honestly, when I first heard the song, I just didn't like it. But as I have reflected on the idea a little more, there is a principle here that is rightly acknowledged, especially in light of Jesus's example. As He enters the garden to wage war, He goes with praise to God on His lips. One might say, as a poet-warrior, fully aware of the intensity of the fight but also reassured through the truth of God's Word that victory is certain.

This brings us back to the description of Jesus being "sorrowful and troubled." What does this mean? Well, for starters, I don't think it means He was merely worried about the physical suffering. Nor can we conclude that Jesus failed to trust God in this moment (1 Pet. 2:23). Neither was it because Jesus did not know what the future held for Him or that He was reluctant to save His people. Instead, I believe Jesus was sorrowful and troubled because He knew what the salvation of His people would cost Him. He knew what it would take to satisfy God's righteous and holy wrath toward our sins. He knew how evil the sins were that He would bear as our sacrifice. Yet He would not be deterred. While sorrowful and troubled, He was also resolved. He entered into the suffering and death that would bring us life with a full awareness of what it would mean. And He did not enter in without the sorrow that we would naturally expect, because while Jesus was and is fully God, He was and is fully man. He not only does for us what we could never do ourselves—save us through His sacrificial work—but He also sets an example for us to follow. When faced with the options between suffering for the sake of obedience to God and avoiding suffering by disobeying God, Jesus's example makes it clear: no matter what obedience to God costs us, it is always right and good, and God will ultimately vindicate us.

While you and I will never face the suffering Jesus faced, it may well be that you are reading this chapter in the midst of suffering, and you are tempted to despair. In your despair, you might be inclined to abandon God completely, or, at the very least, attempt to negotiate a middle road, a third way between obedience and disobedience in order to lessen the impact of your circumstances. I get it. For fallen men, this is natural. Yet our example is not a fallen man. He is a perfect man. And He calls to join Him on the Calvary road. To entrust ourselves to God, who judges justly (1 Pet. 2:23).

Good Gifts from a Gracious God

With the example of Jesus before us, does this mean there are no practical means of common grace that God uses to help us in our despair? While it is important to see that the most crucial aspect of our fight against despair is found in Jesus Christ, we should also note that He provided us with many other good gifts to help us along the way.[4] In addition to entrusting yourself to God, I would also encourage you to consider these good gifts from God.

Fight the Good Fight of Faith Physically

In Paul's two letters to Timothy, he addresses two physical aspects of Timothy's life that I believe are important for us to see. Timothy was most likely a young pastor who struggled with discouragement. In 2 Timothy 2:1, Paul writes, "You then, my child, be strengthened by the grace that is in Christ Jesus." Throughout the rest of the letter, Paul consistently reminds Timothy that suffering in faithful obedience to Christ is to be expected. Paul's call for Timothy to be "strengthened" and his constant refrain to "suffer" makes me think Timothy was prone to feelings of sadness and sorrow. So, what are the two physical aspects Paul addresses in Timothy's life? Answer: exercise and diet.

> 1 Timothy 4:7–8: "Have nothing to do with irreverent, silly myths. Rather train yourself for godliness; for while bodily training is of some value, godliness is of value in every way, as it holds promise for the present life and also for the life to come."
>
> 1 Timothy 5:23: "No longer drink only water, but use a little wine for the sake of your stomach and your frequent ailments."

If you take these two passages together, while it is true that spiritual concerns are of the utmost importance, Paul still has concern for the physical concerns in Timothy's life. The implication of exercise or "bodily training" for Timothy is that it "holds promise for the present life." Regarding his diet, Paul recognizes that the medicinal use of a "little wine" could go a long way to help Timothy with his stomach issues and frequent ailments.

Obviously, Paul was not encouraging Timothy to drink away his sorrows, as many men try to do. Instead, he was appealing to a common practice in the first century to address a physical ailment. A parallel for us would be to avail ourselves to treatments God has provided us for our physical ailments. And one of the most neglected areas for us is our diets. The things we eat and drink impact the way we feel. Thus, as long as we have these bodies, we should take care of them as good stewards. If Paul cared about Timothy's physical being, we should care about ours.

Now, what does that mean for battling things like despair or depression? Obviously not every reader is going to put this book down and go out and join the local gym. Some of you may not even be able to exercise. So, what's my point? My point is that God has so designed our bodies that sometimes there are physical causes behind our emotional distress that can be addressed with lifestyle changes and a better understanding of our physical health.

I offer one example as evidence: a good friend of mine was counseling a woman for several weeks who felt like she was on the brink of a mental breakdown. She didn't know what the problem was. My friend suggested that she visit a doctor. A few days later after her doctor's appointment, she called him to let him know there was no longer a need for them to meet for counseling. While she was at the doctor's office, she found out that she was pregnant. This simple point illustrates that sometimes all we need is a change in our exercise routine, our diet, our rest, our medicine dosages, or our perspective about our health in order to be better equipped to fight the good fight of faith. If this were not true, then I doubt Paul would have even bothered to mention Timothy's physical troubles. So, if you are typically an upbeat and happy person but have recently noticed an unexplainable dip into sadness or despair, I encourage you to make an appointment with your doctor for a general checkup. Get some blood work done, spend some time in the sun, sweat a little, and see if the darkness doesn't lift a bit for you.

At first glance, you may have just read that last paragraph and concluded that I'm telling you to go get a prescription for an antidepressant or an antianxiety medication. Please read the next few sentences slowly and closely. First, I am not a physician. Medical decisions need to be made with medical experts. Do not read what I have written above and conclude that you need to start or discontinue some medication. Second, while it may be advisable to seek some sort of medical treatment for depression or despair, I would also encourage you to do the research and ask your physician good questions about treatments. A few years ago, I went through a season of near-crippling anxiety. I was placed on medication, and it was helpful. However, I didn't want to stay on the medication and asked my doctor to wean me off of it. Why did I do this? It was partly because I found good, peer-reviewed medical research that showed that good diet, exercise, and sleep habits are often just as effective for regulating some of the neurotransmitters in our brains. In other words, I found that if I adjusted some of my habits, I was better equipped to handle the stress in my life. So, when I say, "Go get a physical and speak with your doctor," I'm not saying, "Go get a pill that will fix all your issues." You may or may not need a prescription for a season. I don't know. Regardless of whether you go visit a doctor or not, there are lifestyle changes you can make today related to your diet, your activity levels, and your sleeping that will change your life. God made us this way, so don't neglect your physical body as you fight the good fight of faith!

Fight the Good Fight of Faith Personally

God never intended for you to dwell in isolation. He created you for fellowship with Himself and others. Most of you are familiar with the two great commandments: Love the Lord your God with all your heart, soul, mind, and strength; and love your neighbor as yourself. These two commands reflect our inherent need for relationship.

Feelings of isolation are some of the hardest for those battling depression and despair. I believe that is why Galatians 6:2 is particularly important for us in this regard. It says, "Bear one another's burdens, and so fulfill the law of Christ." We were not made to bear all of the burdens of this life by ourselves. We need one another. I need you to help me bear my burdens. You need me and others to help you. It is a group effort rooted in the grace of God.

But what makes this possible? The gospel of Jesus Christ does! You see, one of the greatest lies the enemy feeds us is that others will not understand our struggles and burdens. We believe they will reject us. They won't accept us. Admittedly, in the world this may be true, but in the church of Jesus Christ, it must never be true. As Ephesians 4:32 says, "Be kind to one another, tenderhearted, forgiving one another, as God in Christ forgave you."

If you are struggling, then I want to encourage you not to fight alone. Find others who will point you to the hope that is in Christ. If you are not already a member of a good local church, find one as soon as possible. You are a vital part of the body of Christ, but how can a body part flourish if it is not joined to the body? If you are able, find a small group at your church to plug into. The point is simple: you need others in your life to help you live. We all do.

Fight the Good Fight of Faith Prayerfully

Psalm 40:17 says, "As for me, I am poor and needy, but the Lord takes thought for me." What a wonderful thought! The Lord of the universe takes "thought" of us in our poverty and need. Because He takes thought of us, we can, as 1 Peter 5:7 tells us, cast "all your anxieties on him." Prayer is warfare. It is battle. In his famous discussion on spiritual warfare in Ephesians 6, the apostle Paul tells Christians to pray "at all times in the Spirit, with all prayer and supplication" (v. 18).

But what about those times when we don't know what to pray? Romans 8:26 says, "Likewise the Spirit helps us in our weakness. For we do not know what to pray as we ought, but the Spirit himself intercedes for us with groanings too deep for words." Prayer is indispensable in the battle against despair and depression. Even when we don't know what to say, we need to get silent before the Lord with our minds focused on Him and allow the Holy Spirit to plead our case before Him.

Leonard Ravenhill said, "Failing here, we fail everywhere."[5] The importance of prayer cannot be overstated. I'll discuss this more in the final chapter, but for now we need to see that we will make no progress without prayer, yet we will see the Lord move mountains in our lives in answer to it. Men, as you fight the good fight, fight prayerfully!

Fight the Good Fight of Faith Purposefully

In the darkness of depression, it is easy to feel as though our life has no purpose. It is easy to believe there is no point to our existence. Yet God tells us otherwise! While the world would like to sell us on the idea that life is all about us, we must reject this notion. Life is not ultimately about you! It is about God. Specifically, it is about His glory.

After considering the vanity of the world, the preacher from the book of Ecclesiastes tells us what this life is all about. In Ecclesiastes 12:13, he writes, "The end of the matter; all has been heard. Fear God and keep his commandments, for this is the whole duty of man." The apostle Paul states it like this in 1 Corinthians 10:31: "Whether you eat or drink, or whatever you do, do all to the glory of God." To glorify God means to reflect the beauty and holiness of God in our words and deeds and to do so in all of life. It is to show others what our God is like.

This means that despite the difficulty we experience, we, by the grace of God, must realize that our ultimate obligation to God is not severed by our situation. Whatever the case, good or bad, making much of God must be our priority. It must be the purpose in all areas of our life.

How do you do this? It begins and continues with a growing understanding of and love for what Jesus Christ has done for us! According to 1 Corinthians 15:3–4, Jesus died for our sins so that we might be forgiven and freed from the penalty of death and judgment we deserve. No matter how bad we perceive things to be in this life, because of the work of Jesus in His death and resurrection, we can be sure they are only temporary.

Therefore, we can live for him because He has died for us. And that's not some cheesy cliché. It is true. Our ability to face trials and sorrow in this life is dependent on the hope we have in Jesus. Whether it is the loss of a job, a cancer diagnosis, the death of a child, or one of a thousand other awful realities, we can be sure that nothing can separate us from the love of God in Christ Jesus our Lord (Rom. 8:39). There is a purpose in our trials and sorrows, even when we do not understand them.

Fight the Good Fight of Faith Patiently

According to Edward T. Welch, "Depression says, 'Surrender!' The message is relentless, and many comply because even when you know that there is a purpose to your suffering, the battle seems too long."[6] Yet, while depression says, "Surrender," God's Word continually says, "Be patient. Persevere. Endure. Hope." Consider the following passages that call us to endure:

> Romans 5:3 (RSV): "More than that, we rejoice in our sufferings, knowing that suffering produces endurance."
>
> Romans 15:4: "For whatever was written in former days was written for our instructions, that through endurance and through the encouragement of the Scriptures we might have hope."
>
> 2 Timothy 2:3: "Share in suffering as a good soldier of Christ Jesus."

> Hebrews 12:1: "Therefore, since we are surrounded by so great a cloud of witnesses, let us also lay aside every weight, and sin which clings so closely, and let us run with endurance the race that is set before us.
>
> James 5:7–8: "Be patient, therefore, brothers, until the coming of the Lord. See how the farmer waits for the precious fruit of the earth, being patient about it, until it receives the early and the late rains. You also, be patient. Establish your hearts, for the coming of the Lord is at hand."

My prayer for you and for myself is that God would work such patience in us by His Holy Spirit that we might endure. We must not succumb to the instant, on-demand society we live in. Growth in this area of our life takes time. It takes perseverance. It takes patience. We are suffering as "good soldiers of Christ Jesus." Because the victory is sure, we hold on.

Chapter 4

MASCULINE STEREOTYPES AND THE KIND OF MAN GOD CHOOSES

When Ron Swanson stated, "I'm a simple man. I like pretty, dark-haired women and breakfast food," my heart rejoiced, as I looked over at my brunette wife with a big smile. I'm somewhat of a stereotypical man. Honestly, it's the way I was raised. I enjoy hunting, fishing, watching mixed martial arts, shooting guns, and playing and watching various sports. I love smoking briskets and ribs in my backyard and find myself increasingly interested in history. I don't feel the need to apologize about that. At the same time, those characteristics don't fully or even sufficiently define what masculinity is.

To get an idea of how much this was a part of my upbringing, one of the first Bible characters I ever learned about was a guy named Nimrod, who was also the namesake of our hunting club down near Desoto Parish in

Louisiana. Almost every weekend I wasn't playing baseball I spent traveling "down home" with my father. I learned to drive on dirty back roads. We shot rifles, planted food plots, looked for deer scrapes, and talked about my dad's younger days. I wouldn't change anything about those days except I wish I had spent more time with my dad. I cherish the memories and lessons I learned. He taught me a lot about being a man but not in the ways you might think.

You see, while my dad taught me about the outdoors, those skills and interests were not the essence of being a man. More than skinning a buck or removing a fish off a hook, my dad taught me to wake up, work hard, love my wife and kids, and tune out the noise of the world. He showed me the value of being a man of your word, even when it hurt.

The Kind of Man God Chooses

If you were picking a leader, what kind of man would you pick? Let me give you two options. First, you have a man who has demonstrated his skill outdoors. He's able to harvest an animal from the field. He's physically strong. A tough man with rough skin covered in hair. And between the two options, he's a little older. Now, he's kind of rash. He doesn't always make the best decisions, but who does, right? Next, you have a man who some might call a "momma's boy." He doesn't care for the outdoors. He's not known for his strength, and his beard grows in patchy. He's got a soft handshake and doesn't look you in the eyes. He strikes you as sketchy, possibly deceitful. If these two guys were standing before you, based on the limited details, whom would you choose to lead?

Let me be completely honest here. I would choose the first option. He's not perfect, but he fits a societal expectation for what a man is, right? But if you haven't already noticed, the first guy described is a lot like Esau, while the second is more like Jacob. Consider how Genesis 25:27–28 briefly describes these two men: "When the boys grew up, Esau was a skillful hunter, a man of the field, while Jacob was a quiet man, dwelling in tents. Isaac loved Esau because he ate of his game, but Rebekah loved Jacob."

At this point, if you think the other aspects of my description of the two men above is misleading, read the whole story. Esau and Jacob are twin brothers, but Esau is a tad older. He's a great hunter, a man of the field. Jacob, on the other hand, is quiet and a tent dweller (that's Old Testament for "indoorsy"). They are both men, but they are very different. Genesis will detail their moral failings in due time, but their different preferences are just that: preferences. As one Old Testament scholar put it, "In their personalities and in their likes and dislikes, Esau and Jacob, though from the same womb, are worlds apart."[1] I hasten to add, being worlds apart in terms of personalities and preferences does not undermine their masculinity. They are both men. One is not inherently better than the other based on these kinds of preferences.

So, whom did God choose? It's got to be Esau, right? He's the older brother, the great hunter, the man of the field? No, it's Jacob. Why?

The answer to why God chose Jacob over Esau is in Romans 9. If you are familiar with this chapter, you probably know that it has been the subject of a lot of debates. My aim, however, is not to explain all the details in Romans 9 but rather to look at what is going on in choosing Jacob over Esau. To do that, though, we've got to have some context.

Romans 9, with Romans 10–11, gives Paul's answer to the question, Why have so many Israelites failed to embrace Jesus as the Christ? In verses 1–5, Paul expresses his desire for his "kinsmen according to the flesh" to embrace Jesus as the Christ. With so many Israelites rejecting Jesus (though not all), Paul defends the sovereignty and goodness of God against those who would question God's faithfulness.

Against the claim that God has failed, Paul declares that the Israelites' rejection of Jesus is not because God's Word has failed (Rom. 9:6). Rather, it is because not everyone who claims to have a relationship to Abraham and the

Israelites is actually "of Abraham" and "from Israel" (Rom. 9:6–7). Paul states this clearly in verse 8: "This means that it is not the children of the flesh who are the children of God, but the children of the promise are counted as offspring."

In Romans 9:9–13, Paul goes on to explain what it means to be "children of the promise." Children of the promise are not defined by the flesh but by faith. This is a crucial point of Paul's argument in the book of Romans (and the book of Galatians). No amount of outwardly, fleshly conformity results in making us children of God. This is what Paul means when, speaking of Esau and Jacob, he writes, "Though they were not yet born and had done nothing either good or bad—in order that God's purpose of election might continue, not because of works but because of him who calls—she was told, 'The older will serve the younger'" (Rom. 9:11–12).

You see, God didn't refuse to choose Esau because he was a "man of the field," nor did God choose Jacob because he was a "tent dweller." God's choice was "not because of works but because of him who calls." In other words, God chose Jacob and not Esau because He is the God who shows mercy to whomever He wills to show it. The mercy of our good and gracious God makes all the difference! It is not through human will or exertion that a man ends up belonging or being useful to God. Furthermore, it is not the natural inclinations or preferences of a man that determine whether God has a purpose for his life. Rather, God makes the difference in the man. I mean, let's be honest, neither Esau nor Jacob, at least as they are described in Genesis 25, is the kind of man we would want our sons to grow up to be like. One was rash while the other was a liar. Yet God's sovereign purpose remained steadfast. God confounded the conventional wisdom of the day, which, when we reflect on it, should humble us. Men, we belong to God, and we are used by God because He, in His sovereign wisdom and freedom, has chosen us to be His children. And, as His children, He fills us with the Holy Spirit that we might be fruitful and useful for His kingdom purposes. And that choice is not based on the kind of personality and preferences we exhibit in this life. The choice is wholly up to God.

The Danger of Stereotypes

Let me be clear: I don't plan to change my personality or my preferences unless those things conflict with God's Word or loving my neighbor. Furthermore, I am not asking you to change your personality or preferences unless they conflict with God's Word or loving your neighbor. Instead, we must be careful not to allow cultural stereotypes to so shape our understanding of manhood that we miss other men in our churches and community. Without going too deeply into it here, there are troubling consequences in our communities and the greater society when we allow this to happen. If we are not careful, we may inadvertently contribute to the gender confusion that abounds in our crazy society. We need to be reminded that, whether we prefer the field to the tent or vice versa, men are men because God made them men. Men will have different personalities and preferences, but those differences are not the essence of their masculinity.

The things you do in the world—whether that's playing football, performing surgery, coding a website, or writing a poem—are not what make you a man. You are a man because God knit you together in your mother's womb as a male who would grow in physical and emotional maturity to be a man one day. With that said, we are called as men to live a particular way in the world that is consistent with how God made us. We are given responsibility to lead in our community, in our churches, and in our homes while acknowledging that not every man will lead in the same way. We are called to be courageous, though some will express that courage on a battlefield while others express it in a boardroom. We should not judge the character of a man based on where and how he expresses such virtues but rather on the basis of whether he expresses them at all.

I've known a lot of manly, outdoorsy guys who are racked with debt from ATVs or are working on their third marriage. Such guys are not known for their self-control. Some never transitioned from being boys to men. They live in a hellish neverland where they never grow up. As some would put it, "They've failed to launch." Refusing to move out of their parents' house, they prefer playing video games and looking at pornography to getting a job, marrying a woman, and establishing their own family. This is partly due to the fact that they have pursued stereotypical activities that many men are free to enjoy (with gratitude to God) while neglecting the greater responsibilities of masculinity that deal with leadership, sacrifice, courage, and self-discipline. They want manlike things without manlike responsibilities.

Furthermore, I've known a lot of "tent-dwelling" guys who lead with integrity, sacrifice for their families, make courageous, principled stands for truth, and maintain a disciplined life of devotion to Christ. But if I were team captain for the church league basketball team, I'd hardly trust them to hold the clipboard. Such men are still valuable to God and His kingdom purposes in the world, even if the world does not value them as "manly men."

Now, if you are reading this book in a small-group setting with other men, don't be the guy who looks over at the other guy after reading that last sentence and jokingly says,

"That's you." As men, we have a tendency to deploy humor to deflect the seriousness of a topic because we, ourselves, are convicted by what's being said. I know I used to be that way. So please, don't be that guy. Work on yourself and encourage others. Don't beat your metaphorical chest as the field guy in the presence of the tent guys just because you are insecure. If that caution doesn't resonate with anyone else, it's a worthwhile reminder for me. I don't want to be the guy who tears down other guys in order to feel more manly. Children do that, not men.

If we want to grow as godly men in the church and in the world, then we must make room for both field men and tent men and every other kind of man in between. We cannot define manhood so narrowly that we only attract the Esaus of the world while the Jacobs languish in isolation because they don't feel like they meet a stereotype. God uses all types of men with all sorts of personalities and preferences for His purposes and glory.

Putting On Christ

In Galatians 3:26–29, Paul writes, "For in Christ Jesus you are all sons of God, through faith. For as many of you as were baptized into Christ have put on Christ. There is neither Jew nor Greek, there is neither slave nor free, there is no male and female, for you are all one in Christ Jesus.

And if you are Christ's, then you are Abraham's offspring, heirs according to promise."

In these verses, Paul is addressing the concept of being "in Christ" or the doctrine of "union with Christ." This is a gloriously complex but vitally important doctrine for us to understand. The phrase "in Christ" and its variations are used throughout the New Testament, especially in the works of the apostle Paul. Conceptually, it is likely related to Jesus's teaching regarding the true vine and the branches we read about in John 15. Jesus is the true vine, and all who trust in Him are like branches that participate in Him, are nourished by Him, and strengthened by Him. And, as Galatians 3:26 tells us, we are "in Christ Jesus . . . through faith," which makes us children of God. Jesus, as the true Son of God, fulfills all that God the Father desired of His children. We need to see the relationship between being "in Christ Jesus" and how that relates to what we read in verse 27, where Paul uses two metaphors to speak of the believer's union with Christ.

First, in language similar to Romans 6, he says we were baptized into Christ.[2] The relationship between being "buried with Christ through baptism into death" (see v. 4) does not refer to a literal action, unless we believe that one ought to physically die when baptized. Water baptism thus points symbolically to the inward reality that is affected by the Holy Spirit who unites us to Christ by faith, which is

Paul's major point in Galatians. We do not participate in Christ through an outward action but through an inward transformation of the heart that is enacted by God's grace through the gospel. This inward change does not come through the law but through grace.

This reality leads Paul to conclude in verse 28 about the transformation that has not only taken place in the hearts of the believers but also in the believing community. Look at what he writes: "There is neither Jew nor Gentile, neither slave nor free, nor is there male and female, for you are all one in Christ Jesus" (NIV). Paul's point here is that the distinctions, which were real distinctions then and continue in some ways today, do not form the basis of our primary identity, nor should they dictate who belongs to the people of God. Paul is not denying that cultural distinctions exist. Neither is he denying that social distinctions exist or that gender distinctions exist. He is simply denying that membership in the people of God depends upon one of these distinctions. The only distinction that matters when it comes to membership in the people of God is faith in Christ Jesus, the true Son of God.

Paul is not saying that all distinctions have ceased to exist or that all distinctions are inherently bad. It was God's idea to create people from every kindred, tongue, tribe, and nation. It was God's idea to create male and female in His image. Yet such distinctions are not what qualifies someone to share in the inheritance of eternal life. Faith in Christ causes us to be children of God and thus inheritors of God's promise, which is why Paul concludes this section with verse 29: "If you belong to Christ, then you are Abraham's seed, and heirs according to the promise" (NIV). Thus, we can conclude that to "be in Christ" means that we "belong to Christ" and that every right and privilege that belongs to children of God belongs to us because we belong to Christ.

To be "a child of God" is synonymous with being "Abraham's seed." Thus, the promise made to Abraham is fulfilled by Christ, who extends the promise of Abraham to all who "belong to Christ" by faith. There are not two peoples of God. There is but one people of God—assembled by the one new man, Christ Jesus: one flock and one shepherd, made up of Jews and Gentiles (Eph. 2:14–15; John 10:16).

Hence, we find the reason Paul says these earthly distinctions, while true at some level, are not what fundamentally defines our relationship to God. It is our relationship with Christ that has changed our relationship to God.

What does this mean for us as men? It means that "being in Christ" must shape the way we think about being a man. As men, we have a responsibility to lead in our homes and in our churches. Being in Christ does not erase these responsibilities, but it does transform them.

As we saw with Jacob and Esau, the kind of man God chooses to use is not always the kind of man we would pick. In fact, as 1 Corinthians 1:26–31 tells us, God often chose the "foolish things of the world to shame the wise" (NIV) and "the weak things of the world to shame the strong" (NIV). Why does He do this? "So that no human being might boast in the presence of God" (1 Cor. 1:29). Men, if we would boast, let our boast be in Him and what He has accomplished for our salvation on the cross (Gal. 6:14). Let us be men who have put on Christ by faith! But what exactly should that look like? What kind of men should we be?

How Are We Doing, Men?

I love playing golf. I've played since I was in seventh grade. When I started, my brother, Chris, always encouraged me to simply progress the ball down the fairway. Any progress was better than no progress. We didn't keep score. We just played. There was something special about the simplicity and enjoyment of not taking score. However, until I started taking score, I never knew where I stood in relation to the expectation of good golf. The scorecard was an indicator. It told me where I stood in relationship to par on the course. Scorecards are good for us. We have them in sports, but we also have them in other aspects of our life.

The scorecard tells us how we are doing and helps us know where to improve.

When I think about what kind of men we should be, it is helpful for us to know what God expects of us. And when I think about what God expects of us, among other places in Scripture, I think of Hebrews 13. After detailing the faith of saints who went before us in Hebrews 11, and then issuing a call to run hard after Christ in Hebrews 12, the author of Hebrews closes his sermon with an exhortation on how to live until the day we meet Jesus face-to-face. So, for our purposes, you can think of Hebrews 13 as a kind of scorecard to help you evaluate how you are fulfilling God's expectations for you as a man.

Now, with that said, I want to stress that neither I nor the author of Hebrews is saying that we "become Christians" through a certain behavior. We can only become Christians by being born again by the work of the Holy Spirit. By grace alone through faith alone in Christ alone, we are justified before God. We are declared righteous. We are proclaimed to be participants in the kingdom of God. We are told that we are members of God's family, the church. We do not get into God's family by good behavior, nor do we remain a part of His family by good behavior. From beginning to end, we are saved totally by Christ.

But how do men know that they have been saved by Christ? How do we know who belongs in the family? How do we tell who is a participant in the kingdom of God? We can know that we are saved, that we belong in the family, that we participate in the kingdom of God by considering the fruit of our lives. This is what Jesus said in Matthew 7:15–20 and what Paul encouraged us to do in 2 Corinthians 13:5. But to do this, we need a scorecard to guide us. Hence, Hebrews 13:1–25 is a great place for us to look as it reveals the scorecard by which the Christian man can judge his life in accordance with God's Word.

In Hebrews 13:1–3, Christians, men included, are called to love one another. In fact, the author refers to "brotherly love" here. This reminds me of Jesus's statement in John 13:35, where He says, "By this all people will know that you are my disciples, if you have love for one another." What a statement! People will know we belong to Jesus by the way we love one another. By the way we love our enemies. By the way we love the weak, wounded, and oppressed in our midst. Men, do people know you belong to Christ because of your love for others? Isn't it interesting that Jesus doesn't say they will know you are my disciple by how you attend church, talk about church, or give to the church? Faithful Christian men certainly do such things, but it is by their love that they are known. Men, how are we doing with loving others? Would your wife, your children, or your fellow church members describe you as the kind of man who lets "brotherly love continue"? And this is not "love" in word only but also in action. Hebrews 13:2–3 makes this point by giving an example of how this brotherly love is expressed in hospitality toward others. Men, let us love God and our neighbor as those who have put on Christ.

A second test for us as Christian men is our sexual purity. Hebrews 13:4 puts it this way: "Let marriage be held in honor among all, and let the marriage bed be undefiled, for God will judge the sexually immoral and adulterous." The verse is straightforward enough—honor marriage by highly regarding the purity of the marriage bed. The phrase "marriage bed" refers to the monogamous, heterosexual relationship of one man and one woman in the context of a lifelong, covenantal union before God. In no uncertain terms, the author is speaking about the need for sexual union to be enjoyed and celebrated in the context of a marriage that honors God. Faithful Christian men do not downplay marriage. They lift it up! They celebrate it! They defend it! They teach about it! They encourage others to partake of it!

Marriage is not the subject of a faithful Christian man's joke or coarse jesting. Marriage is not something to be derided. Your wife is not the "ol' ball and chain" or someone to belittle to make yourself feel big. Marriage is not the end of your freedom or the demise of your youth. It is a blessing from a loving God who intends for your marriages to point others to Christ's relationship with the church. Men, how are you doing in honoring your marriage? Are you fleeing sexual temptation? Are you keeping the marriage bed pure? Faithful Christian men will honor the sanctity of marriage.

In Hebrews 13:5–6, the exhortations move from marriage to money. Here we learn that faithful Christian men will hope in God instead of their wealth. No amount of wealth will ever be able to save you or bring the peace verse 6 brings us when it says, "The Lord is my helper; I will not fear; what can man do to me?" Wealth can be stolen from us. Our health can be here one day and gone the next. Yet Jesus Christ, the One who is the same yesterday, today, and forever, tells us, "I will never leave you nor forsake you" (v. 5).

Jesus is emphatic about His willingness to never leave us or forsake us. Wealth cannot make such promises! Health cannot give us such security. Only Jesus can make such promises to us! Only Jesus is worthy of the hope we often misplace in wealth and health. Yet, how often do we men get distracted by our pursuit of money and success? As I've told you before, I struggle with worry and anxiety. And if I'm being honest, it's often about family finances. There's nothing inherently wrong with wanting to take care of your family. In fact, Scripture teaches us that we must take care of our families (1 Tim. 5:8). We are providers, and we should not take that responsibility lightly, but we mustn't let a responsibility become an idol that takes our focus off God or our family. We must balance the desire to provide with the realization that God is ultimately the One who takes care of us and our family (Matt. 6:25–33). We must not put our trust in things of this world but in God. Men, how are you doing with your relationship to money? Do you view it as something to be treasured in itself or as a tool to be used for God's kingdom?

The next section (Heb. 13:7–19) of the scorecard deals with our willingness to submit to godly leadership. It begins by encouraging us to consider our leaders and follow their example. Our leaders should set a righteous example for us to follow in obedience to Christ, which refers to pastors in the local church. Pastors have a tough job. "Not many," according to James, "should become teachers" of God's Word (James 3:1) because they will be held more accountable. This goes for the lives of pastors as well. They are called to give us an example to follow, as are other leaders past and present. The object of your imitation is to be the faith of your leaders. Even the pastors you follow should have leaders whose faith they want to imitate. You should aspire to live a life that is governed by faith, which according to Hebrews 11:1–2 is "the assurance of things hoped for, the conviction of things not seen." How can we have assurance of the things we hope in? We must place our hope, our faith, in the unchanging Christ, as Hebrews 13:8 tells us: "Jesus Christ is the same yesterday and today and forever." So, while your leaders may be susceptible to failure and falling in their daily walk with Christ, Christ was not and is not susceptible to failure. You can trust in Him. Pray for your leaders that they might model such faith in Christ and that you will model such faith as well.

Related to this idea of submitting to godly leadership, we are warned to beware of false teachers. If we would follow righteous examples, then we must find examples of those who were sold out to the truth of Jesus Christ. This is what verses 9–16 are all about. We must not be led astray by "diverse and strange teachings," especially as they relate to our faith in Jesus. If you notice in the verses that follow verse 9, the author is concerned with false doctrines that undermine faith in Jesus by adding to the gospel of Christ. Some teachers were telling people they needed to eat certain foods and to abstain from others in order to have a deeper fellowship with God. We are "strengthened by grace," not by keeping man-made religious observances. If Jesus had finished the work the Father had given Him by becoming a sacrifice for us, outside the camp, bearing all our guilt and shame away, then there was no need to turn back to the former ways of life that undermined our full allegiance to Jesus. Jesus is enough! So, as we submit to our leaders, we do so in so far as they teach and model truth for us. We are, however, under no obligation to follow a leader whose teaching or life contradicts and undermines what we have been taught in God's Word. On the contrary, such leaders should be resisted and removed from leadership in our churches. And men, you have a major role to play in that work. You should hold leaders accountable as faithful members of your local church.

Now, having said all of this about following the example of godly leaders, then seeing that we also have a responsibility to resist ungodly leaders, we now circle back to our need to submit to the leadership of godly leaders in the church. We see this in verses 17–19, which teach us that faithful Christian men will obey, submit to, and pray for their leaders.

I'll be the first to admit that this point was always hard to preach and teach when I was a pastor because it could be viewed as self-serving. I mean, a pastor telling his congregation that they need to obey, submit to, and pray for him? Really? Well, given the fact that no Scripture ever came by the will of man but by the inspiration of the Holy Spirit, I, and your pastors, have a divine obligation to teach you God's Word, and unless Hebrews 13:17–19 is not God's Word, it must be taught and observed. So, as far as your leaders follow Christ, Christ expects you to obey the things they have commanded you to do from God's Word, submit to their leadership, and pray for them that their ministry might be fruitful.

The passage teaches you not to cause your leader's labor to be joyless or full of groaning. A joyful pastor who enjoys his ministry is a blessing to the church he leads under the authority of the Great Shepherd, Jesus Christ. A pastor who consistently feeds the sheep, leads the sheep, knows, and protects the sheep is a good thing for the church, even if some people don't understand this principle. A pastor works for God, not a church. Pastors may come and go as the Lord sees fit to move them to different flocks at different seasons. But whoever is the pastor, if he is feeding God's people the unadulterated Word of God, protecting them from error, loving them in the truth, praying for them regularly, and seeking to lead them in holiness, the church should obey them, submit to them, and pray for them. The church that does not do such things for a faithful pastor is inflicting harm upon itself.

Men, if you would follow this instruction, it will require humility from you. How are you doing in this respect? Do you pray for your pastor? Or do you ridicule him? Do you make his work better or harder? How are you supporting the leaders God has placed over you? Maybe you are reading this right now and the Spirit of God is convicting you of some sort of rebellion or bitterness that you have harbored against your leaders. If so, why not take a moment to pray for your pastor and reach out to him and let him know that you did? You might never know how far a kind word will go in his life today.

Finally, we come to verses 20–25, where we are taught that godly men will desire to be equipped to do God's will. While it may seem awkward to some to hear someone talk about the church's responsibility to the pastor as their leader, those who want to be equipped to do God's will won't feel awkward about it at all. The faithful Christian man wants to be fed, challenged, and equipped for every good work. This was the author of Hebrews's prayer for his people. That was the reason he wrote the book of Hebrews in the first place. The point was not to expound on all this great theology for the sake of knowing more without action. The point was for the people to be equipped for godly action. He wanted them to live according to the truth of the gospel of Christ. He wanted their lives to look different. He wanted them to live by a different scorecard.

Conclusion

So, how is your scorecard looking? Have you found some areas you can pray about? Has the Lord revealed some things in your life that need to change today? If He has revealed such things to you, thank Him. He reveals our areas of need in order to heal us, not in order to condemn us. He doesn't expose the cancers in our soul to make us sorrowful and full of despair. He exposes the sickness to bring about a full healing. He is faithful to answer the one who asks, so ask Him to make you a more faithful Christian man whom He is delighted to use for His glory and the good of others.

Chapter 5

RETRIEVING THE SEXUALITY THAT THE WORLD HAS STOLEN

I'm ashamed to admit it, but I'm pretty sure the first full book of the Bible that I read of my own volition was the Song of Solomon. Why the Song of Solomon? Well, as a prepubescent boy, something about that book felt forbidden. The Song of Solomon is a type of writing called poetic wisdom literature in the Old Testament that "describes both marriage and God's relationship to His people."[1] When speaking of marriage, the author is not ashamed of the intimacy between a husband and a wife. To be sure, the Song of Solomon is not vulgar or inappropriate, nor is it tame. The book speaks of passion, jealousy, love, and commitment. There is a sanctity to the sexuality it describes. Of course, when I first read the book, my naïve, unbelieving eyes turned God's good gift of sex to married couples into a shameful matter. Why did I do that?

Despite my parents' best efforts, I learned about sex from a much older kid in the neighborhood (dads, as a general principle, don't let your elementary school kids hang out with eighth graders). My friend's dad kept *Playboy* magazines around the house, which he was eager to bring out and share with all the other kids. So, when my parents did finally take me to the church library to retrieve an age-appropriate book about sex, I had to feign ignorance and interest. You probably know the kind of book I'm talking about. One of those "how your body is changing" books. Unfortunately for me and my parents, those cartoons in the Christian book didn't grab my attention like my neighbor's *Playboy* did. Thus, anytime I encountered sex, even when I read about it in my Bible, I filtered it through a pornographic lens. In this way, the world stole from me a sense of what God intended for sexuality. If that was the case for me at such a young age, how much worse must the robbery be for young boys and men today? My encounter required knowing another kid whose dad was shameless enough to leave magazines around the house. Nowadays, pornographic content seeks all of us via the phones in our pockets.

As Christian men, we live in a world that is hostile to the holy sexuality we are called to embrace. So, as you read this chapter, my hope is that the truths contained in it would, with complete dependence on the Holy Spirit, take back some of the territory the enemy has stolen in our life. To do this, let's consider what God's Word and the world say about sexuality and consider how the world deceives us when it comes to sex.

What Does God's Word Say about Our Sexuality?

Asking this question assumes God has revealed His intention for human sexuality. The theological category used to describe God revealing His intentions to humans is called *revelation*. Within this theological category, there are two types. First is *general revelation*, which is available to all people by observing creation and the order of the world. The second type of revelation is *special revelation*, which depends on God's initiative to reveal Himself to us. For our purposes, special revelation means what we read in the Bible. We will look at general revelation in the next section, but we'll begin with what God has revealed about human sexuality in the Bible.

At this point, we must acknowledge that acceptance of God's truth depends on a work of God's grace in a person's life. We need to be given "eyes to see" and "ears to hear" (see Matt. 13:16). In our flesh, we do not accept the things of God. We need the Holy Spirit to illuminate our darkened hearts (John 16–17). Why is this important to acknowledge? Because if we think convincing others is a matter of providing a better argument, we will be sorely disappointed. Even when we make strong, compassionate arguments for God's truth—and we must—we still need God to move in each life before being able to receive these truths. That happened to Lydia when the apostle Paul preached in Philippi (Acts 16:11–15). The Lord opened her heart to respond to Paul's message. We need our hearts opened. Even as I write this chapter, I am praying He will open our eyes to see His truth more clearly.

Let's begin at the beginning. Genesis 1:26–31 and 2:4–25 reveal God's ideal for human sexuality. God created male and female in His image for the purpose of being fruitful and multiplying, subduing the earth. The context in which man and woman were called to be fruitful was marriage. Marriage is the union of one man and one woman in a marital covenant before God. This is the paradigm. Sex in marriage is God's idea. He designed it. He could have made humans differently, but He chose a particular way. He gave us the capacity for procreation and pleasure in the context of marriage. This ultimately exists for His glory and our good. Sadly, as we saw earlier, sin marred the good thing God created. In time, God's Word would spell out certain rules for our sexuality that safeguard God's good intention for sex.

As the story of Scripture progresses, we quickly see how sin steals God's intention for sexuality from us. Just a few chapters after the account of the creation and fall of humanity, we see sex move outside of God's intention with Lamech taking two wives. Jesus confirms that God's plan for marriage was one man and one woman for a lifetime (Matt. 19) when he argued with certain religious leaders about marriage. Lamech's example shows that sin distorts our understanding of sexuality and leads to all sorts of problems in society. Admittedly, things appear to get a little weird in the account of the Nephilim in Genesis 6 that describes the "sons of God" engaging in sexual acts with the "daughters of man," which results in the emergence of "mighty men." It is possible these "mighty men" were giants like Goliath, whom we see later in the biblical story.[2] Among the many interesting details that emerge from this passage, one principle remains true: when sex is removed from the context of marriage between one man and one woman, things go badly.

As the story continues, God spells out rules for His people in the Mosaic covenant He made with Israel. They are for the good of His people. In the law of Moses, instances of sexual immorality are forbidden, including sex outside of marriage (Exod. 22:16–17), adultery (Exod. 20:14), prostitution (Deut. 23:18), incest (Deut. 22:30), homosexuality (Lev. 18:22), cross-dressing (Deut. 22:8), rape (Deut. 22:25–29), and bestiality (Deut. 18:23). This is not an exhaustive list of prohibitions within the Mosaic covenant, but they give us a feel for what God's design is for our sexuality.[3]

When we move into the New Testament, we find Jesus, the new Moses, affirming the aspects of the Mosaic law, which are not related to the things He would fulfill in His role as the Messiah (Matt. 5:17–20). Jesus was not afraid to appeal to the Mosaic law to ground God's vision of sexuality. Furthermore, we see Jesus getting at the heart of what the Mosaic law pointed Israel to all along. In Matthew 5:27–30, Jesus situates our sexual thoughts, desires, and acts in the context of marriage. In Matthew 15:19, Jesus speaks clearly about the sinfulness of sexual immorality. When He does, He assumes the categories of heterosexual marriage, which is the only kind of marriage God recognizes (Matt. 19:1–12). Furthermore, Jesus celebrates marriage in John 2:1–11. He also implicitly condemns perverse actions like pedophilia and all forms of child abuse in Matthew 18:1–14. In Revelation 2:14 and 20, he warns the seven churches in Asia about tolerating sexual immorality. Jesus rightly says many strong things about sexual immorality. Yet, for those who are guilty of it, He offers hope for forgiveness if they repent of their sins and trust in Him (Matt. 21:31–32). To those outside the core Jewish people in His day (Gentiles), He often spoke with care in the course of the correction (John 4:1–26).

Jesus, however, is not the only New Testament person to speak about sexuality. Paul addresses sexual immorality on multiple occasions, condemning all forms of sexual immorality as a perversion of God's intention (Rom. 1:26–27; 13:13; 1 Cor. 6:9–11; 6:18; Gal. 5:19, Eph. 5:3, 1 Thess. 4:3; 1 Tim. 1:8–11). But Paul is not all condemnation. Like Jesus, Paul celebrates marriage as God intends it (Eph. 5:22–33) while offering hope to those who repent of their sins (1 Cor. 6:9–11).

One important thing to note is that Paul, like Jesus, did not think that engaging in a sexual relationship was essential to personhood. In other words, having sex is not what makes you a "real man," or even human for that matter. We are, as men, designed with a nature that includes sexuality. By this I mean that our bodies are designed for sexual union. Men who desire marriage should do so and enjoy the blessing of sex as God has intended it. Yet, not all men may end up married, or they may end up widowed.[4] One thinks of men like Charles Simeon, who dedicated his life to ministry as a chaste single man.[5]

While the decision to embrace chaste singleness for the sake of ministry is exceptional, that does not mean it is somehow dysfunctional or that such men are not truly men. Likewise, men who choose not to remarry after the death of their wife are no less men simply for choosing to remain unmarried. Jesus, the greatest man who ever lived, did not marry or engage in sexual activity.[6] Surely, we would not impute to Jesus some sort of defect simply because He was not married or a virgin. Don't buy the lie that says to be a "real man" you must be sexually active. Sexual activity may be something men do in the context of their marriage, but boys don't become "real men" by being sexually active. A man living in chaste singleness is not less of a man. If he desires to be married, he should pray that God would provide him with a wife and seek by grace to live as the kind of man a godly woman would desire to marry. Yet single men should not be regarded as second-class men in the kingdom of God.

Among what other biblical authors taught about sexuality, the author of Hebrews warns about God's judgment for sexual immorality (Heb. 12:16; 13:4). Peter instructed Gentile Christians to abstain from sexual immorality (Acts 15:20), and Jude condemns sexuality and perversion (Jude 7). In the last book of the Bible, John records what Jesus revealed to Him regarding those who are fit for the inheritance of God's kingdom (Rev. 21:8).

God's Word—that special revelation—says a lot about how to live in a world that has been broken by sin, especially as it relates to our sexuality. All this instruction is aimed at safeguarding the goodness of God's good gift of sex for His glory and our care. As the Creator of our sexuality, He sets the boundaries because He knows what's best for us and the world we live in. But is there any indication from that world that these things are true? The world, warped by humanity's sin and rebellion, often distorts the good things God made. However, that is not always or universally the case. Sometimes the world serves as a witness to the truthfulness of God's Word. That witness is what we refer to as general revelation.

What Does the World Communicate about Our Sexuality?

While Scripture is the ultimate guide for our understanding of sexuality, it is not the only guide. The natural world, which relates to general revelation, complements what God's Word teaches about biblical sexuality. Stated another way, there is continuity between what the Bible teaches and what we can observe about the world even apart from the Bible (that's special revelation). Two passages of Scripture are helpful for understanding this idea: Psalm 19 and Romans 1.

In Psalm 19, specifically verses 1–6, David tells of how creation itself is revealing God's glory. He says, "Day after day [the heavens] pour forth speech; night after night they reveal knowledge" (v. 2 NIV). David's point in this psalm is that God is revealing Himself through creation. God has embedded revelation of His character into the created world. Thus, even while sin has distorted aspects of this revelation, there remains a testimony to God in the natural world through the created order.

While Psalm 19 is speaking generally about the glory of God we see in nature, it has implications for our understanding of our own creatureliness, specifically as it relates to our bodies. Many of the perversions and problems the church is facing regarding sexuality are rooted in a misunderstanding of this creatureliness. To quote Timothy Tennent, "The church has failed to understand that seemingly disparate issues regarding sexuality (same-sex marriage, gender reassignment, adultery, pornography, cohabitation, abortion) are actually manifestations of a single root problem—namely, our failure to articulate a Christian view of the body."[7]

As ethicist Oliver O'Donovan stated it, "To have a male body is to have a body structurally ordered to loving union with a female body, and *vice versa*."[8] I don't have to spell this out for you. Let the reader understand and rejoice.

In Romans 1, specifically verses 18–20, the apostle Paul reinforces the point made in Psalm 19 regarding the testimony to God in the world. In fact, the testimony of God is so clear in the created world that all inhabitants of the earth will be held accountable before God for either acknowledging or rejecting what can be clearly known about Him in creation. Paul writes, "For since the creation of the world God's invisible qualities—his eternal power and divine nature— have been clearly seen, being understood from what has been made, so that people are without excuse" (v. 20 NIV).

In terms of how the testimony of God's world relates to the question of sexuality, we must continue reading in Romans 1, where we are told that those who have rejected God's revelation of Himself in creation have been given over to their idolatry; and, as a result, they were given "over in sinful desires of their hearts to sexual impurity for the degrading of their bodies with one another" (Rom. 1:24 NIV). Paul goes on to describe this degradation in Romans 1:26–27, saying, "God gave them over to shameful lusts. Even their women exchanged natural sexual relations for unnatural ones. In the same way the men also abandoned natural relations with women and were inflamed with lust for one another. Men committed shameful acts with other men, and received in themselves the due penalty of their error" (NIV).

As these verses make clear, "natural relations" were embedded into the order of creation that men and women were abandoning because they refused to acknowledge God and His design as He had revealed it in the world.

We will look at this in a little more detail in the next section, but for the moment we need to see that God's Word points us to a testimony of God's design for sexuality that has been revealed in God's world. In other words, the vision of sexuality we see in God's Word is confirmed by physical, biological, anatomical, genetic realities that are undeniable in our world. Yet, when people deny God and His ordained ordered in creation, they turn to a perversion. They exchange the truth of God for a lie.

The Context for Our Sexuality: Marriage

In His great wisdom and kindness, God has ordained that sex be enjoyed and honored in the context of marriage (Heb. 13). When a man leaves his parents and is united to his wife, the two become one flesh (Gen. 2:23–25). Within that context of marriage, man and woman, before God and others, commit themselves in vows to each other. A promise is being made. A promise that is far more important and consequential than the promise you make when you tell a bank you will repay the mortgage or the car loan. It is a promise to God, before God, and to another bearer of God's image. Only in this context of promise can the powerful act of sex flourish. For, it is only here that the act is safe because of how the act is intended to function. Now, what do I mean by "how the act is intended to function"? I mean that God's design in the body is reflected in the ways our bodies respond to the sexual act.

Let me explain. God has designed our bodies to be so interconnected with one person that when we engage in a sexual act, hormones are released that bind us to the person with whom we are engaging in the act. Hormones like oxytocin (primarily in women, which has been called the "attachment hormone") and vasopressin (in men, which has been called the "monogamy hormone") because of the way they are released and create feelings of attachment to others. This is true of nursing mothers with babies, and it is true of people who are engaging in sex. In other words, God has written biochemical attachment into our bodies for sex. And, as a result of this, when we engage in so-called "no strings attached" sex, we are actually lying to ourselves, but we are, in reality, creating a chemical bond to others.[9] God made us to bond with those with whom we have sex.

But there is more to this union than initially meets the eye. Our marriages are telling a story (or at least they should be) about Christ's relationship to His church (Eph. 5:21–33). Within such a marriage, God has appointed the husband to lead and love with a sacrificial concern for the total well-being of his wife. This is not just physical and material well-being, though it is certainly not less! The husband should care for his wife as he does his own body, just as Christ does for the church. Likewise, the wife should submit to and respect her husband, just as her husband and the church submit to Christ.

I get that this is not popular in our present society, but faithfulness to God's Word is not a popularity contest. Misogynists don't like the call to sacrifice and care for one's wife. Feminists don't like the call to submission and respect for one's husband. Scripture teaches both. And both are easier to envision when both are present. Husbands who sacrifice and care for their wives are easier to submit to and respect, and vice versa. But this is not a book for both spouses in a marriage, so men, here is what I'd say to us: the call to lead and love our wives well is a call to die daily. You're not responsible to make her submit to you. If she rebels against God's Word in this regard, if she is one of His children, she will face His discipline, just as you will face His discipline if you do not lead and love your wife well. You're going to have to make sacrifices to make your marriage last. Not sacrifices in terms of convictions about God's truth but personal sacrifices about your own personal comfort and ease. Why is this worth it? Paul tells us in Ephesians 5:32, "This is a profound mystery—but I am talking about Christ and the church" (NIV). It's worth it because such a marriage is part of God's plan for displaying His glory in the world!

The Thief that Comes to Steal, Kill, and Destroy

As we have already seen, when sexuality is removed from its God-given context, devastating things happen. At the core of the sexual revolution was the idea that sex could be isolated from covenant relationship before God and others. Sex was simply an act to be enjoyed in the body. It became an expression of an idea of love that was rooted in culture instead of God's design. We don't have to look much further than the creation of the birth control pill and the right to abortion to see how awry things go when we abandon God's ideal. With the potential for procreation removed from the picture of the sexual relationship, individuals could seemingly live unburdened of responsibility and risk and sleep with whomever they desired. All of this was touted as freedom; yet what the movement did not realize (or failed to acknowledge) is that one cannot separate the action done in the body from the impact it has on a person's soul. To put it another way, while the claim was that the sex of the sexual revolution came with "no strings attached," the aftermath demonstrated that there was simply no such thing as "no strings attached" sex.

How did we get here? We got here by attempting to divorce our bodies from our understanding of self. This idea, which is often called "body-self dualism," has led to the argument that "what you do with your body sexually need not have any connection to who you are as a whole person."[10] Yet the connection between body and person is inescapable. God created sex not only for our pleasure but also as an expression and physical actualization of union between one man and one woman in the context of marriage. Tim Keller said, "Sex is God's appointed way for two people to reciprocally say to one another, 'I belong completely, permanently, and exclusively to you.'"[11]

Now, remember what I said about this biochemical union that occurs in sex; it makes sense that the only context in which that union is right and good is the context of marriage. Otherwise, we are simply going around making promises with our bodies to people we do not intend to keep nor can keep because we have not committed our lives to them. And when we do this, the results are devastating. Our brains are wired for intimacy, but when we circumvent intimacy in favor of promiscuity, our brains and bodies get sick. As Anne Maloney put it, "It is no coincidence that the top two prescribed drugs at our state university's health center are antidepressants and the birth-control pill."[12] We were not made to hook up. We were made to bond. We were made to know and be known. Note how when the sexual act is mentioned in the Bible, it is often described as spouses "knowing" each other (Gen. 4:1). The term *yada* carries connotations of a deep, personal way of knowing. And the context for such *deep knowing* is marriage, where a promise before God and others is made, an anatomical union of bodies is promoted, and the potential of a family is present. Tragically, sexual immorality seeks to sever this bond in all sorts of different ways.

Take, for instance, pornography. Hardly anyone can live unaffected by pornography in our day. From the magazines at our children's eye level in the grocery store checkout line to the potential sewer pipe of Internet connectivity we carry in our pockets, the ubiquity of pornography plagues our society. For decades, many argued that pornography was harmless. Like the arguments bolstered in favor of the sexual revolution, pornography use was claimed to be safe. Yet, in more recent days, as brain scientists have started studying things like neuroplasticity, it has become obvious that pornography is enslaving and punishing our society.[13] From the dehumanizing exploitation and harm of men and women in the porn industry to the fundamental devaluing of sexual intimacy in marriage to the porn-induced physical, emotional, and psychological issues facing thousands of people, we are learning that we do not consume pornography; pornography consumes us.

People might argue, "But who is really getting hurt? The people who are participating in pornography are doing so because they want to." Or, "Isn't it better for me to watch pornography than to go out and actually have sex with someone?"[14] Here's the thing: people are harmed by pornography. The participants in it, the producers of it, and the consumers of it. In terms of participants in it, there are near countless testimonies of former participants who have walked away from it because of the mental and physical abuse they experienced. This is not even to mention the fact that many "participants" in pornography are not willfully doing so. Many are victims of sex trafficking. They struggle severely with depression, being more prone to substance abuse and suicide. This is true of many involved in the production of pornography as well.

In terms of those who consume pornography, there is a physical and emotional toil. Men who watch pornography are twice as likely to divorce.[15] Other research has demonstrated that porn actually shrinks the brain.[16] There is also compelling evidence that pornography is addictive (like a substance) given how the hormones in the brain react to the stimuli of pornography. One example of this is porn-induced erectile dysfunction, which is when an otherwise healthy male is no longer able to have sex with real women because porn has so warped his understanding of sexuality and the nude form that he is no longer turned on.

When we remove sexual arousal and consummation from its covenantal context of monogamous, heterosexual marriage, we exchange "natural relations for those that are contrary to nature."

> God did not intend for our sexuality to be synthetically consummated in front of

> a magazine, stage, or screen. Sexuality is not a commodity for the consumption of the masses. Such an understanding of sex is contrary to nature. When this truth is exchanged for the lie, sex is no longer about our worship of God, but rather, it is about our worship of sex. And as we pervert God's natural design for sexuality, we begin to receive in ourselves the due penalty of our error.[17]

Pornography is just one example, but it is a big one. I doubt that any man reading this has made it this far unscathed by pornography. I mention it not to heap guilt and shame on you but rather to expose the disease of our sin to the Great Physician who came so that we may "have life and have it abundantly" (John 10:10).

Conclusion

Because of Christ, there is hope. Hope not only for our forgiveness but also our restoration. You see, Christ is plundering Satan's kingdom, setting captives free. While aspects of your sexuality may have been stolen by the world, with its "desires of the flesh and the desires of the eyes and pride of life" (1 John 2:16), "we have an advocate with the Father, Jesus Christ the righteous. He is the propitiation for our sins, and not for ours only but also for the sins of the whole world" (1 John 2:1–2). Because of Christ's atoning death on the cross, where He went to war for our souls and laid down His life in our place, we can be free. We don't have to let the world keep what it has stolen. We can enjoy a redeemed sexuality that is rightly ordered for God's glory and our good.

Chapter 6

FATHERS WHO POINT TO THE FATHER

On June 27, 2022, my father passed away. He was eighty years old. As a son and a pastor, I had the privilege of speaking at his funeral two days later. While my dad was a Christian, he wasn't the type of Christian people write biographies about or would have invited to speak at a men's retreat. His faith was simple but genuine. He trusted Christ, taught Sunday school for a season, and faithfully attended church. He wasn't, however, much of a reader. His bookshelves were not full of theological writings. He liked mafia stories, probably because my late uncle Ben—and his brother-in-law—was an FBI agent tasked with driving out organized crime on the Gulf Coast decades ago. Our conversations mainly dealt with real life. He would get mad at times, but I don't ever remember a night when he didn't walk by my bedroom door and tell me that he loved me. He was a provider, but that was not always easy. In fact, he worked right up until the weekend he had a stroke and never came home again. He had tough hands from hard work but a tender heart. As he got older, he cried more often or at least more publicly. He had an infectious laugh and a great sense of humor. He taught me how to hunt, how to fish, and how to drive.

He was a good father. I knew this while he was alive, but it wasn't until after I said goodbye to my dad that I realized there is a grace about having a good father that helps us trust our heavenly Father. My father was a good father by pointing me to the Father in ways he probably didn't even realize at the time. This shouldn't surprise us when it happens. Jesus even addressed it in his famous Sermon on the Mount.

The Grace of a Good Father

In Matthew 7:7–11 (NIV), Jesus teaches about the nature of God's kingdom. In those verses, we read,

> Ask and it will be given to you; seek and you will find; knock and the door will be opened to you. For everyone who asks receives; the one who seeks finds; and to the one who knocks, the door will be opened.

> Which of you, if your son asks for bread, will give him a stone? Or if he asks for a fish, will give him a snake? If you, then, though you are evil, know how to give good gifts to your children, how much more will your Father in heaven give good gifts to those who ask him!

In verses 7–8, Jesus calls His disciples to a life of persistent prayer undergirded by the promise that those who ask will receive, those who seek will find, and those who knock will have the door opened for them. The promise of an answer compels us to keep praying with our asking, seeking, and knocking. What are we to ask, seek, and knock for? Jesus has already told us in Matthew 6:9–13 (NIV). When we pray, we are to pray like this,

> Our Father in heaven,
> hallowed be your name,
> your kingdom come,
> your will be done,
>   on earth as it is in heaven.
> Give us today our daily bread.
> And forgive us our debts,
>   as we also have forgiven our debtors.
> And lead us not into temptation,
>   but deliver us from the evil one.

In this prayer Jesus's disciples ask their heavenly Father to make His name great, higher than all other names. Then, Jesus speaks about the Father's kingdom coming on earth as it is in heaven, which is to speak of God's saving reign through Jesus in the world through the gospel proclamation. Only after the hallowing of God's name and the priority of His kingdom's advance does Jesus's model of our daily prayer turn to our needs, which consist of our daily sustenance, our need for forgiveness, and deliverance from temptation.

These are things Jesus promises we will find and receive as we ask and seek in obedience to His command, which we encountered in Matthew 7:7–8. Each of these things is worthy of much more consideration and reflection, but what does this have to do with good fathers? I am considering Matthew 7 in this context because I believe this passage points to one of the greatest legacies any good father could ever leave his family. When Jesus intended to encourage his audience to continue asking, seeking, and knocking, He appealed to their fatherly instinct. Notice again what Jesus said in Matthew 7:9–11 (NIV), "Which of you, if your son asks for bread, will give him a stone? Or if he asks for a fish, will give him a snake? If you, then, though you are evil, know how to give good gifts to your children, how much more will your Father in heaven give good gifts to those who ask him!"

Did you catch that? In building his case for why His disciples could have assurance in their prayers, Jesus essentially says, "Even you fathers who are sinners know how to treat your children well! Even you fallen fathers know enough goodness that when your children ask for bread, you give them bread. When they ask for a fish, they get a fish. And if this is the case, then how much better, and greater, and more glorious will the blessing of our heavenly Father be, who gives gifts to those who ask Him!"

The implication here from Jesus's instruction is that fathers, though not perfect—in fact, evil compared to God—ought to serve by example to assure their children of the goodness of their heavenly Father. This is what we could call an argument from the lesser to the greater. If earthly fathers hear and respond to their children's needs, then how much more will our heavenly Father listen to us and respond to our request.

As I grew up, I saw this example repeatedly in my father. As I've already said, my father was not perfect. Those who only ever imagined my father as a gentle, soft-spoken soul who would never get upset had obviously never tried to take his order at a drive-through speaker. His imperfections were not hidden from those who knew him best. Was Dad gentle at times? Of course. Soft-spoken? With his granddaughters, always. Perfect? No way. A sinner? Yes. Like the rest of us. Yet, even as a sinner, he knew goodness, and he was generous with his goodness toward his family and so many others.

The Lie Bad Fathers Tell

As I grew up, I saw God's goodness in light of my dad's goodness, but I also came to see that not every dad was like my dad. Not every dad would have heard Jesus's instruction in Matthew 7:9–11 and thought, *Well, of course, fathers are just supposed to hear the needs of their children and respond accordingly.* Some fathers in our day would hear Jesus's instruction, and it would find no place in them. Some fathers treat their family in such a way that when their family members hear God called "Father," they are not reassured but horrified. I recently spoke with a person who mentioned this problem to me. We were studying praying to God as our Father, but I mentioned that we must be careful not to project all aspects of our relationships with our earthly fathers back onto our heavenly Father. This person told me that praying to God as Father had been difficult because of the abusive way their earthly father had treated them. They thanked me for clarifying and differentiating God as Father from abusive earthly fathers. Yet, even still, the story broke my heart. This is not how God designed fathers to be, but in a fallen world, all is not as it should be.

Some fathers do not take care of their families; instead, they care for themselves. Some fathers are more committed to their hobbies than their homes. Some fathers are abusive. Such fathers, humanly speaking, functionally undermine their children's faith in the goodness of our Father in heaven because the image of a father they show their family is not in keeping with the image of our heavenly Father. Bad fathers tell lies about our good Father in heaven through their words and actions.

As a father, I need to hear this. I can have all my theology "right." I can make sure we have nightly family devotions. I can teach my children the catechism. I can teach them hymns, psalms, and spiritual songs. I can discipline them. I can tell them the importance of love and generosity. But if I am not habitually embodying the same ideals I am teaching them, then I am undermining their faith in the goodness of God. If I tell them to respect their mother while I disrespect her as my wife, they will see through me. They will perceive my instruction and discipline as mere expressions of my parental power and dominance, arbitrary rules and regulations that make them more bearable to be around but do not aim to see their hearts enflamed for God. Instruction and punitive discipline unhitched from spiritual formation are just propaganda and abuse by another name.

And this is where I find my own father's most significant legacy: Ronald Hough never spoke, acted, or treated his family in a manner that made it hard for us to believe that our Father in heaven was good. In fact, my dad cared for, loved, supported, and celebrated us in such a way that it was almost unfathomable that we could be more cared for, more loved, more supported, and more celebrated by our heavenly Father. And he did it with a relatively rudimentary understanding of the Bible, no large theological books on his bookshelf, and never attending a conference on fatherhood or parenting. He was a simple man with a simple faith striving by God's grace to provide for and love his family well to the end.

And this is, at least partly, what Jesus was getting at in Matthew 7. With all our sins and imperfections aside, earthly fathers should point their children to the magnificent glory of our heavenly Father through their words and actions. In other words, when I think of my dad—his love, his commitment, and his goodness toward my family and me—first, I ought to thank God for such a father. Second, I ought to think, *If my earthly father was this good, how much better must my heavenly Father be.* And so He is!

It is a blessing of God's grace to have read Matthew 7:9–11 and never thought, *My dad didn't know how to take care of his family. So why should I trust God?* No, I read that passage and immediately thought, That's exactly right.

Ronnie Hough never got asked a question from one of his family members that he wasn't willing to answer if he knew the answer. If there was a need my father could meet, he would meet it. He would sacrifice his own prosperity to watch his family flourish. He answered every phone call his failing ears ever heard from his youngest son, even if it was just a question about whether I needed to buy 13-13-13 or 10-10-10 to spread in my front yard or how to load the muzzleloader he loaned me. He was always willing to help, whether it was working on a vehicle or a riding lawn mower or helping me board up broken windows at a rental property.

Such a vision of fatherhood is both terrifying and freeing. It is terrifying to see the relationship between a father's words and deeds and how their children will perceive God as Father. There is more at stake than just raising children. We are orienting our children to God by the way we speak and the way we act. And when there is a sustained disconnect between what we expect of our children and how we ourselves actually live, we unwittingly undermine their trust in God as a good Father. This is not the legacy we want to leave our children. D. A. Carson stated, "The worst possible heritage to leave with children: high spiritual pretensions and low performance."[1]

But in this terrifying vision of fatherhood, there is also freedom. As Jesus's own example acknowledges, earthly fathers are sinners, and as sinners, they need God's grace. This means we do not parent out of our perfection but out of the grace the good Father has extended to us in Jesus Christ. We don't have to act like we have it altogether as parents. We don't have to have all the answers. We don't have to be perfect. We simply need to be good enough by God's grace to point our children to the greater goodness of God as our Father who cares and provides for all of us. This means that, as fathers, we need to be willing and ready to confess our sins when we have wronged our wives or our children. Furthermore, this means our parenting should be marked by generosity in all sorts of varieties.

My dad was never rich according to worldly standards, but that never stopped him from giving generously to those in need and blessing his family with meals and vacations. He was just happy to watch all his family spend time together. Even when things in his company were hard, and that was often—owning your own business is not for the faint of heart—or his health was uncertain, and I am sure Dad struggled with his own doubts at times, my dad never undermined my faith in the goodness of our heavenly Father through his words or deeds. My dad was generous with his love, his forgiveness, and his encouragement. When I was stressed out, dealing with my own anxiety from school and ministry, Dad spoke simple but reassuring words, saying, "God's going to take care of us. There's no need to worry, Bud."

My dad might have been imperfect, but he was also exceedingly good to his family. And we regard this as a gift of God's grace. Good fathers are God's grace to His people. And good fathers help us believe that God's grace is good. Of all the things I could say about my father, and of all the things I will remember about him, and all the things I aspire to emulate, I want to be the type of father that when my family reads Matthew 7:7–11, they will walk away with a more profound assurance in the goodness of their heavenly Father, because even their earthly father knew how to take care of them. I want them to think, *Wow, if my earthly father was this good to me, how much better must my heavenly Father be.*

Longing for Fatherhood

But what about men in the church who long for fatherhood but either have not experienced it yet or may not experience it as they had hoped? Well, one of the first things we need to acknowledge is that fatherhood is a category all men, even if they are not currently fathers, have feelings about. Even if a man's father was not a good father, they are only able to make that assessment based on the fact that they have some conception in their mind about what a good father is. This is one of the things we see in Jesus's example about fathers. He assumed the category of fatherhood was applicable to His audience. So, whether you are currently a father or you are longing for fatherhood, the category of father is still important. We, as followers of Christ, through adoption by the Holy Spirit, relate to God the Father as His children. We have an idea of what it means to have and be a father.

But what about the men who are longing to be a father? I believe such men can still model for others what it means to be a man who cares for others with fatherly concern. We see this exemplified in the spiritual language Paul uses to describe his ministry to different churches in his letters. While Paul was not Timothy's biological father, he related to him as a spiritual father. He cared for him. He encouraged him. He supported him. He even corrected him, in a fatherly manner, regarding his propensity to timidity. And he did all of this without having a biological relationship to Timothy. Surely, if Paul could relate to Timothy this way, older, more mature men in the faith can relate to younger men in the church. Just consider Paul's instruction to Timothy about the ordering of the church in Ephesus and how it reveals that biological relationships are not the only ones in which a fatherly relationship can exist.

So, for the men who are longing to be fathers, biblically speaking, there is no need to feel they must wait until they have biological or adopted children to demonstrate these fatherly instincts. Furthermore, churches serving in our society will doubtlessly have boys and younger men who need a father figure. Fatherlessness is a scourge in our society. Why not step up and into this role in your local church? Why not show a generation of boys growing up without fathers in their homes what it means to be a man who serves and sacrifices like Christ? If you are thinking, *But where do I start?*, I would encourage you to reach out to the leaders in your church, get vetted and trained through their safety protocols (which, if they do not currently have, insist they establish them), and then start serving as unto the Lord!

The Poet-Warrior Father

When I think about how the image of the poet-warrior fits within this vision of fatherhood, I think about my father's hands. Even in old age, my father had tough, strong hands. He worked hard. He was strong, but I never recall my father working out except for walking around the neighborhood after his heart attack. He loved to garden and work on small engines. He played basketball until his freshman year of college but quickly realized he could not balance his schoolwork and the demand of being a student athlete. So he prioritized getting his education and providing for his young family.

For a man who I never recall seeing lift weights, he seemed strong as an ox. Those tough hands loaded chemicals into the back end of customers' trucks for decades. Yet, for all of his toughness, he used his hands to care for his family. I still remember having a terrible stomach bug in high school that left me severely dehydrated. I was so weak I could not reach the car in my own strength, but I was nearly a full-grown man. My dad was nearing his sixties, but that did not stop him from cradling me and carrying me to the car to head to the emergency room. His strength was a source of comfort for me. Those tough hands, which would have gone to war for my family and me if needed, did not mean he had to be a hard man. There was a tenderness in his toughness. And that is where the poet-warrior is seen in fathers.

As we saw in the example of Jesus, the poet-warrior is strong enough (and willing) to turn over tables and gentle enough to be approached by children. The poet-warrior father is strong, but the strength is not used to abuse or be domineering but to nurture and defend his children. He disciplines, and his discipline is not pleasant, but neither is it punitive or angry. He exercises his fatherly authority with the aim of formation, praying that his children would become and be faithful followers of Jesus Christ. He speaks with gentleness and understanding to his wife yet seeks relentlessly to protect her from all that would aim to harm their marriage. The poet-warrior sees through the false intimacy promoted within society, whether through pornography or other forms of sexual immorality. He buffets his body, bringing his passions into subjection to the will of God for his sanctification by the empowering work of the Holy Spirit. He leads his family through services and sacrifice, taking his cues from Christ, who is the source of his life.

One doesn't need an advanced seminary degree to be this type of father, but instead, a continual filling of the Spirit of God. The life I am describing here is filled with the fruit of the Spirit. It is a life that depends on God's grace in Christ. It is not a life that can be lived apart from God's empowering mercy and forgiveness. Earthly fathers will often fail to pursue such a life, but this is no cause for despair. God's grace is sufficient, even for fathers.

When we think about the role of the father in a family, I think we need to be reminded of this reality. Fathers will not be perfect. They need God's grace like the rest of their family. We would do well to remind fathers that amid their God-given responsibilities, there is also God-given grace to sustain and restore them. And as God's grace sustains and restores them, good fathers play an invaluable role in pointing their children to the Father.

Chapter 7

THE RHYTHMS OF A POET-WARRIOR LIFE: DESIRE, DISCIPLINE, ACCOUNTABILITY, CONSISTENCY

For the past five years, roughly four days a week, my friend Eric Nimtz has been at my home. Unless you are fortunate enough to be one of his close friends, you probably don't know Eric. If you had ever met him, you'd probably remember him. He is affectionately known as "loud Eric" around these parts. He's got a big personality and a passion for seeing people grow in all areas of life. I got to know him first as his pastor and eventually as his friend. We connected over our shared love of smoked food and Jesus Christ. Beyond that, we didn't have a ton in common.

Eric is a former college athlete. He played defensive end in college and still lifts ridiculous weights in my garage, which has been dubbed the "pain cave" due to its rugged aesthetics and poor air circulation. You just don't know hot until you have lifted weights in a Houston summer without a fan! I, on the other hand, was a competitive junior golfer with no real prospects of playing beyond high school. The only lifting I did in high school was to tote my golf bag around the course. After high school, I became somewhat of a professional student, completing four different degrees, while currently working on a fifth. If one were to chart where we are on the poet-warrior spectrum, I am more the poet while he is more the warrior. That's not to say that Eric is not academically inclined. He is an engineer after all. But our paths in life were different. Yet despite those differences, there we were, some five years ago, in the pain cave, lifting weights and studying biblical interpretation together. He taught me how to dead lift while I taught him how to diagram a passage of Scripture.

In time, my three sons got interested in working out. Eric, being the guy he is, started investing in them along with a group of their friends. Day in and day out, for the past five years, they have gathered in that garage for strength training. My oldest son, who once could hardly walk in a straight line due to being born with a clubfoot, now regularly lifts more weight than his father could ever hope to lift. I've still got a video on my phone of the first time he attempted a back squat. It was awkward and looked painful. Now, at least at the time of this chapter, he can nearly back squat four hundred pounds. Such transformations have become common in the pain cave. All the young men who have stuck to the program have grown immensely. They are all bigger, stronger, and faster than they were five years ago. It's been fascinating to observe, especially considering where they all started.

As I watched these young men grow in their physical strength and stamina, it caused me to reevaluate how I think about my devotion to Christ, especially considering how often the Bible draws parallels between athletic imagery and the Christian life. There are no overnight successes in the physical gym or the spiritual gym. If we would grow as God intends, a holy effort—a spiritual sweat of sorts—is required.

To be sure, this does not contradict the apostle Paul's warning to the church in Galatia. Paul was dealing with a group of false teachers who were attempting to add to the finished work of Christ for our justification. Justification is the doctrine that teaches that we are declared righteous before God on account of faith alone, which unites us to Christ. False teachers were teaching the Galatians that they needed to be circumcised to be justified before God. Paul rightly challenged this false understanding of the gospel of Jesus Christ. We are saved from start to finish by grace through faith, and this is not of ourselves, but "it is the gift of God" (Eph. 2:8). Make no mistake about our salvation: "having begun by the Spirit," we will not now be "perfected by the flesh" (Gal. 3:3). We are truly saved by faith, yet our faith is a living faith. And it is a faith that grows as the Spirit works in us. And God, in His grace, by making us a new creation (2 Cor. 5:17), intends for us to work out our salvation in "fear and trembling," for God works in us, "both to will and to work for his good pleasure" (Phil. 2:12–13). In other words, if your understanding of God's grace in Jesus Christ makes you think you can be apathetic to spiritual growth, you have deeply misunderstood.

In this chapter, I want to share some of what I have observed in God's Word and encourage you in your pursuit of Christ, including some practical suggestions. I want you to be strengthened by grace (Heb. 13:9) to work hard at your spiritual growth.

Desire and Discipline

If you've read the New Testament at all, you've likely seen the imagery that is often employed to describe our spiritual life. One thinks of passages like 1 Corinthians 9:24–27, which says,

> Do you not know that in a race all the runners run, but only one receives the prize? So run that you may obtain it. Every

> athlete exercises self-control in all things. They do it to receive a perishable wreath, but we an imperishable. So I do not run aimlessly; I do not box as one beating the air. But I discipline my body and keep it under control, lest after preaching to others I myself should be disqualified.

The apostle Paul starts this passage with the rhetorical question, "Do you not know . . . ?" The anticipated response is, "Of course we know, Paul." So, what do they know? They know that "in a race all the runners run, but only one receives the prize." I guess there were no participation trophies or bronze brackets in ancient Corinth. This imagery reinforces Paul's point at the end of verse 24: "So run that you may obtain it!" But what will the runner obtain? Unlike the earthly runners who received a perishable wreath, runners in this heavenly race receive an imperishable wreath. In other words, an everlasting reward. Furthermore, while only one earthly runner receives the prize, a multitude of heavenly runners will receive the imperishable wreath.

While Paul does not expand on the substance of the "imperishable wreath" in this passage, given what we see in 2 Timothy 4:7–8, where Paul speaks of his own race, I believe we can conclude that he has "the crown of righteousness" in mind. This is the reward set before all

Christians who run the race of faith to the end. We are called, as Hebrews 12:1–2 tells us, to "run with endurance the race that is set before us, looking to Jesus, the founder and perfecter of our faith." It is not enough to start the race and then stop. We must continue to run the race to the end where we are assured of the "crown of righteousness."

As we set out to grow as followers of Christ, we must do so with a desire and discipline empowered by the Holy Spirit. I saw this firsthand with my sons and their friends. Eric regularly preached the need to cultivate a desire for growth that was tempered by discipline. The discipline—meaning consistency and repetition—safeguarded the young men from being completely driven by their desire or lack thereof. This is important because there will be times when the work required to grow physically or spiritually is hard. The John Piper influence in my life might have me say, "We don't desire God as we know we ought."[1] as we know we ought. But does this mean we simply stop showing up, stop reading our Bibles, stop praying, or stop gathering with God's people in the local church because we "just don't feel like it today"? Surely this is not the kind of men we aspire to be. We keep showing up and putting in the work on good days and tough days. We "discipline [ourselves] for the purpose of godliness" (1 Tim. 4:7–8 NASB).

Let me give you an example. When I was younger, most churches still had a weekly prayer meeting. Ours was on Wednesday nights. Admittedly, it was tough to get home from work, eat supper, get the kids ready, and make it to those meetings. The easier option was to just stay home. However, I cannot tell you how many times I went to prayer meeting out of discipline and ended up being blessed beyond measure. I left many of those meetings unburdened by the prayers of my fellow church members and the work of the Holy Spirit. I was filled with joy and refreshment in Christ. The discipline of gathering with God's people led to joy, even when the joy was not initially present. Discipline meant making sacrifices to grow. The discipline strengthens the desire.

To be sure, this is no "pull yourself up by your bootstraps" Christianity. We are fueled by the gracious acceptance we have before God in Christ. But we also need to see that the fuel of God's grace works to produce a holy, Spirit-empowered effort that produces a spiritual sweat, of sorts, that aims to run the race. We must avoid the implications of Paul's imagery in 1 Corinthians 9:24–27. Anyone who has ever run a race or been in a boxing match or rolled on a jiujitsu mat or attempted strength training knows that some sacrifice and pain are involved. As Paul Gardner notes in his commentary on 1 Corinthians,

"Prizes must be worked for, and the way is hard and humbling and painful."[2]

This vision is one of passionate runners who want to finish the race set before them. They have a desire that compels them to run, but this same desire to run also constrains them to lay aside the things in their life that encumber them. Hebrews 12:1–2 speaks of this need to lay aside "every weight, and sin which clings so closely" as we "run with endurance the race that is set before us," as we look "to Jesus, the founder and perfector of our faith."

With each of the above passages, we note the role that discipline or "self-control" plays in our progress. Desire is not enough. Just as the desires of our New Year's resolutions rarely carry us through to life change, so also our desire for spiritual growth needs discipline.

So, what does it look like to cultivate a more disciplined life for the spiritual growth we desire as Christian men? Let me make a few simple suggestions. First, you need to be a committed member of a good, biblically faithful local church.[3] It's fine for you to listen to sermon podcasts by your favorite preachers, but those men are not your pastors. You need to sit regularly under the authority of biblically qualified pastors in a local church (1 Tim. 3:1–7). Any spiritual disciplines you integrate into your life will only supplement the work God is doing in you through the ministry of His church. If you are not committed to a local church, make it a priority to find one as soon as possible.[4]

Once you are plugged into a local church, I think the other forms of spiritual disciplines have more of an impact on your spiritual growth. For instance, you should be regularly meditating on God's Word. As David declares in Psalm 1:1–2, "Blessed is the man who walks not in the counsel of the wicked, nor stands in the way of sinners, nor sits in the seat of scoffers; but his delight is in the law of the Lord, and on his law he meditates day and night."

A good local church will help you grow in this area as you hear God's Word preached every week. A good pastor will help you read your Bible better by faithfully preaching God's Word to God's people. Thus, your daily meditation on God's Word will be an overflow of your weekly gathering with God's people in the church. If, however, you are not sure where to begin with your own meditation on God's Word, I suggest getting a good translation of the Bible that is easy for you to read. Additionally, if you can afford it, pick up a study Bible like the ESV Study Bible or CSB Study Bible, which will provide some explanatory notes to passages with which you might not initially be familiar.[5] If you have a commute for work or just prefer to listen to God's Word being read by someone else, then I would recommend an app like Dwell. It is a wonderful audio Bible app that gives users a lot of different translation and voice options. All of this is to say that you need to be committed to getting God's Word in you, and there are now many ways to do that regardless of your schedule and learning preferences. Whether you are reading or listening, be sure you are meditating on God's Word as you encounter it.

Alongside meditating on Scripture, you need to be a man of prayer. As Paul taught the Christians in Thessalonica, "Pray without ceasing" (1 Thess. 5:17). Obviously, Paul was not encouraging these believers to abandon all other activities and retreat to a monastic life of prayer. Instead, he was teaching them that prayer was to be as much a part of this daily life as eating, drinking, and breathing. As one of my pastors used to tell us, "You are never too busy to pray. You are too busy not to pray." If you are wondering how to pray, you'll find a list of resources at the end of this chapter that I recommend, which have helped me immensely.

Okay, so, we have the spiritual disciplines of commitment to the local church, meditating on Scripture daily, and ceaseless prayer. Is that it? Well, of course not, but these are the lifeblood of your spiritual growth. To draw the parallel to physical training again, I would say these three disciplines are the core exercises. They are the press, squat, and dead lift of spiritual growth. While there are other disciplines to practice, they should be supplemental to the regular practices of being a committed church member, meditating on God's Word, and praying regularly throughout the day. The other disciplines, which you can learn about in the recommended books at the end of this chapter, will do you the most good if you are regularly practicing these core disciplines. Don't neglect these core disciplines. They will provide the foundation upon which all other spiritual disciplines can flourish.

Now, you may be saying, "This list is great, but I'm just not a disciplined person. I don't have a lot of desire. What should I do?" I'm glad you asked, and don't be ashamed about admitting your struggle. This is where the next two aspects of our spiritual growth come in.

Accountability and Consistency

If our desires and discipline are going to bear the most fruit in our lives, then they need to be supported by accountability and consistency. In fact, accountability and consistency are inextricably related to the cultivation of desire and discipline. Take accountability for example. Imagine that you want to start a strength training or a nutrition plan to get healthier. You start the plan, schedule reminders in your calendar, buy the meal prepping boxes, and for a few weeks, things are going well. Then life happens. You sleep poorly one night so you tell yourself, "I'm not going to go to the gym today." Then you have a lunch meeting at work, and none of the menu options fit into your nutrition plan, so you splurge. Typically, this results in a cycle of shame and guilt, which spirals out of control. You feel like a failure; therefore you just embrace it and tell yourself you will start again next Monday or maybe next year. Sound familiar?

Maybe this doesn't sound familiar in terms of your physical health, but how many among us can say that each year we commit to reading through the Bible and praying every day and have never failed to fulfill this spiritual aspiration? Few of us can say, "I've never failed to fulfill what I have aspired to do." But oftentimes this is because we have sought to undergo a spiritual transformation in isolation from other believers who will hold us accountable and encourage us to be consistent. We need one another if we are going to grow into the men God calls us to be in the world.

Accountability comes in various forms. First, and most foundationally, accountability ought to be an everyday part of our lives as members of a local church. God has set up His church to provide accountability for God's people. Galatians 6:1–2 makes this clear: "Brothers, if anyone is caught in any transgression, you who are spiritual should restore him in a spirit of gentleness. Keep watch on yourself, lest you too be tempted. Bear one another's burdens, and so fulfill the law of Christ." We are called to be burden-bearing brothers to one another. Furthermore, we should be open to the kind of accountability that restores those who wander from Christ "in a spirit of gentleness." Men, do you have other men in your life who will restore you when you wander from Christ and bear your burdens? If not, then you lack biblical accountability, and your soul is in danger. If you cannot receive correction from others, you need to humble yourself and submit to godly leadership in the church for the sake of your joy in Christ.

Such accountability might come in the form of one-on-one discipleship, or it may be found in a small-group setting at your church. And while it is great for you to have a good relationship with your wife that spurs you on to love and good deeds, you also need to have relationships in the church with other men who point you to Christ and hold you accountable to the faith you profess. If you think you are too important or too successful to have accountability, then you are the kind of man whom Paul warns against in Galatians 6:3: "For if anyone thinks he is something, when he is nothing, he deceives himself." Don't deceive yourself into thinking that you don't need accountability.

But what about the relationship between accountability and spiritual disciplines? When I think about this question, it reminds me of the power of expectations. Several years back, I got involved with a CrossFit group at my local YMCA. I know, I know, you think I was in a cult, and to be sure, there were certainly some interesting people in that group. With that said, during that time, I got into the best shape of my life. Why? Was it because of the superiority of CrossFit as a program? I don't think so. It was because every day I knew a group of people expected me to show up and work out. And if I didn't show up, my phone would light up with text messages checking on me. The high expectation of showing up and putting in the work made me want to show up. There was a communal pressure to be there, and I think that is why it worked so well for me. In more recent years, the CrossFit routines have given way to more traditional strength training in my garage. And instead of a large community of people who were expecting me to show up, it was just my friend Eric. He showed up day after day to lift with me. And the result was that I got stronger. Why? It wasn't because the strength training plan was better than every other program out there; it was because I showed up and put in the work.

Now, imagine that instead of physical exercise, you develop a relationship with another brother in Christ who is committed to holding you accountable to your commitment to spiritual disciples. Maybe you meet for coffee each week or enjoy breakfast with each other at the local Waffle House to talk about your commitment to your local church, your meditation on God's Word, and your prayer life. You know the questions are coming each week. And, unless you are an unrepentant liar, you know you have holy work to do. Week in and week out, you are being held accountable as you hold others accountable, and slowly but surely, you are growing into the man God has called you to be, which leads us next to consider the importance of consistency.

Over the years, I have heard people say, "We tend to overestimate what we can accomplish in a year and underestimate what we can accomplish in a decade." I think this is particularly true not only in our pursuits for physical health but also our spiritual health. While a whole aftermarket of people claim they have found the "secret" to physical or spiritual growth, desperately trying to sell it to you, the reality is that the only surefire way to grow in anything is by consistency. Notice that I did not say *perfection* here. You don't have to be perfect to grow physically or spiritually, but you do need to be consistent. This means there will likely be days when you can't make it to church or meditate on God's Word or pray as you would like. Sometimes you will start Bible reading plans and get derailed for a few weeks. The goal here is not to quit. Don't give up. Don't let some momentary failures keep you from getting back to this holy work. As Proverbs 24:16 teaches us, "For the righteous falls seven times and rises again, but the wicked stumble in times of calamity." Man of God, when you fall, get back up.

Now, I'm not suggesting that real, substantial change cannot happen in an instance with regard to our spiritual health. I'm reminded of a story I read by John Piper. Piper wrote,

> Many have heard of the Great Welsh Revival of 1904–1905. It touched all classes and ages. Newspapers kept tally as the churches swelled with new converts—over 100,000 in one six-month period. In Cardiff police reported a 60 percent decrease in drunkenness and 40 percent fewer people in jail at the New Year of 1905. In Glamorgan the convictions for drunkenness decreased from 11,282 in 1904 to 5,615 in 1907. Stocks of Welsh Bibles were sold out. Profanity was so diminished in the coal mines that the pit ponies dragging the coal carts in the tunnels did not understand their commands any more and stood still, confused. Even children held their own meetings in homes and barns.[6]

In a sovereign work of the Holy Spirit, many people were instantly changed. God's Spirit still moves in this way. However, we must also recognize that while certain habits of sin may stop immediately when we are converted, lingering sins also need to be put to death (Col. 3:5). This is where accountability and consistency factor into our spiritual growth as men. Find men who will hold you accountable and strive for consistency in the core disciplines God has ordained for our good and His glory.

Christ Our Example

As you already know, this book seeks to consider Christ as the perfect example of what it means to be a man. But this chapter has mainly been about our own spiritual efforts to grow. Where is Jesus in all of this? First, we see that Jesus was a man of perfect discipline. Jesus's custom was to rise early in the morning for prayer (Mark 1:35), and He is often seen reading and teaching the Scriptures to groups of people (Mark 10:1). If Jesus, God in the flesh, had a habit of regularly engaging in prayer and reading Scripture, then how could we ever assume that such habits are beneath us? Second, while Jesus was perfectly sinless and incapable of sinning, nonetheless, He developed close relationships with His disciples. This is not to say these disciples held Jesus accountable or made sure He was being consistent, but rather Jesus taught that His disciples need one another.

Jesus taught us about the need for accountability in passages like Matthew 18, where those who refuse to repent of sin should be held accountable by others in the church. Furthermore, by means of His parables, Jesus taught us the value of consistency, like the sower who sowed seed among the different types of soil (Matt. 13). This parable draws on the imagery of one who consistently sows the seed of the gospel among various people. How could anyone expect a harvest of souls if they are not consistently about the work of sowing the seed of the gospel? So, while there is a uniqueness to Jesus's humanity that nuances the parallels in important ways between Him and us, there is still an example to be followed here. And for those who may have read my admonition about the importance of being in the local church with cynicism or skepticism, just remember that Christ died to save His bride, the church. To have little to no regard for the church is to mock the work of Christ who died to build His church.

Regardless of where you find yourself on the spectrum of the poet-warrior continuum, you need God to cultivate a desire for growth in your heart that is safeguarded by spiritual discipline, accountability, and consistency. The warriors among us will likely welcome the call to discipline but shrink back at the thought of accountability in the local church. Sometimes accountability can feel like a threat to a man's independence. And, in a sense, it is, but that is not a bad thing. As I've said before, there are no lone rangers or self-made men in the kingdom of God. You need accountability.

The poets among us will appreciate the importance of desire while not always liking the idea of discipline. Discipline means there are boundaries to our affections, which is also a good thing. We need self-control, lest our wayward desires consume us.

Doubtlessly, other men are caught somewhere in between these two horizons. But each of us needs to understand that we have not been called to embark on this holy work alone. You need other men in the context of the church to help you bear the burdens you are facing as a man. Christ died not only to save you from the wages of sin but also that you might have an abundant life of spiritual growth in conformity to His image (Rom. 8:29). We need to have our minds renewed according to God's will (Rom. 12:1). Therefore, don't wait to start this journey in spiritual growth. Don't delay until next Monday or next year. Start now, and by the power of the Holy Spirit working within you, cultivate and live a life worthy of the gospel of Christ (Phil. 1:27).

CONCLUSION

Men, we are called to live differently in the world. Yet we live under constant pressure to conform to ideals that are contrary to Christ and His will for our lives. In this book, I hope you have caught a glimpse of the vision of masculinity to which God has called you. It is a call for courageous faith in and obedience to Christ. It is a life of sacrifice for others. A life of responsibility and self-control. Not that you may be regarded as healthy, wealthy, and wise by the world but so that you might honor God above all. To do this, we need the balance of the poet-warrior—modeled after Jesus—who reflects and feels deeply about the things that matter most and who fights with an intensity equal to what is at stake in our families, our churches, and our communities. At times, you may feel more the warrior than the poet, or vice versa, but I encourage you to remember what you have witnessed in Jesus Christ, the perfect man who is the only mediator between us and God (1 Tim. 2:5).

Over the course of this book, we have seen Jesus express the whole range of sinless emotions as a fully human man. We considered the sinfulness of apathy and the need to fight the good fight of faith in the midst of the despair. God's Word has taught us that while the world has certain agendas for masculinity, God's design is better, even when it is not popular. We have learned that as real Christian men we love our wives and our kids, work hard without idolizing our work, take care of ourselves so that we may have a body fit for being a living sacrifice, to guard ourselves from sexual temptation, and submit to godly leadership in the context of the local church while protecting the church from false teaching. Real Christian men don't need thousands of followers on social media or millions of dollars in the bank to be used by God. We just need to be captivated by Christ, willing to suffer for doing good, and full of hope for the future.

At times, just like the tires on our vehicles, we will find ourselves out of balance. We will drift from one side of the poet-warrior paradigm to the other. When we drift too far to the poet side of things, we become so introspective and caught up in our emotions that we find ourselves paralyzed, unable to do the work to which God has called us. When we drift too far to the warrior side, we become more like wild animals than men, using our strength to destroy and roam according by our passions to our own demise.

In such times, we must return to Jesus, looking to Him as the "author and perfecter of our faith" (Heb. 12:1–2 ASV). And as we run to Him, we run with Him, seeing that,

> Jesus also suffered outside the gate in order to sanctify the people through his own blood. Therefore let us go to him outside the camp and bear the reproach he endured. For here we have no lasting city, but we seek the city that is to come. (Heb. 13:12–14).

In running with Him, we will come to realize that some of us experience triumphs of faith like Abraham and Moses (Heb. 11:8–31) while others face the fates of those mentioned in Hebrews 11:35–38:

> Some were tortured, refusing to accept release, so that they might rise again to a better life. Others suffered mocking and flogging, and even chains and imprisonment. They were stoned, they were sawn in two, they were killed with the sword. They went about in skins of sheep and goats, destitute, afflicted, mistreated—of whom the world was not worthy—wandering about in deserts and mountains, and in dens and caves of the earth.

You see, being a man doesn't mean you always look victorious in this age. Those who follow Christ will not always have it easy, but that's not why we follow Him. We follow Him because He's worth it. Whatever we lose in order to follow Him is worth it because He's worthy of all our poetic affection and warrior effort. He laid down an example for us to follow, and He filled us with the Holy Spirit to equip us for good works as His workmanship (Eph. 2:8–10), even when we face trials and tribulations in this life.

As Christian men, we must remember Christ's promises to the seven churches in Asia, found in the book of Revelation. While He corrects them where they have erred and calls them to repent, as they faced the persecution for the faithfulness to Christ, He reminded them that those who trust in Him will conquer the evil one (Rev. 2:7, 11, 17, 28; 3:5, 12, 21). But how will they do it? Will they defeat the evil one by taking up arms? By deceitful schemes or by amassing wealth or political power? No. We will not conquer through the weapons of warfare that the world values. As Christian men, we wage war differently from the world.

How then will we conquer? Revelation 12:11 tells us, "And they have conquered him by the blood of the Lamb and the word of our testimony, for they loved not their lives even unto death." We win in this spiritual warfare by embracing the hope of the blood of Jesus and testifying to the work of Jesus, even amid trials and tribulation. It is not by comfort and ease that the enemy of our soul is defeated; it is through faithfully enduring tribulation and trials as true witnesses to the goodness and grace of Christ that our enemy is ultimately overthrown. And as we wage this war, we do so with the song of the Lamb on our lips, declaring,

> "Worthy are you to take the scroll and to open its seals, for you were slain, and by your blood you ransomed people for God from every tribe and language and people and nation, and you have made them a kingdom and priests to our God, and they shall reign on the earth." (Rev. 5:9–10.

Men, this is the life we have been called to live. Deeply reflective and fully resolved as whole men, made in the image of God, for His glory and the good of others. This is the vision of masculinity we need to retrieve, not the counterfeit versions we see on every corner. Resist the temptation to be shaped by the world. Instead, heed the apostle Paul in Romans 12:1–2:

> "I appeal to you therefore, brothers, by the mercies of God, to present your bodies as a living sacrifice, holy and acceptable to God, which is your spiritual worship. Do not be conformed to this world, but be

> transformed by the renewal of your mind, that by testing you may discern what is the will of God, what is good and acceptable and perfect."

If Christian men heed these instructions, balancing our lives with the example of Christ—the perfect man—our families, our churches, and our community will be blessed beyond what we could ever ask, think, or imagine. God intends to use you for His purposes in the world, as a poet-warrior being conformed into the image of Jesus Christ.

RECOMMENDED RESOURCES ON SPIRITUAL DISCIPLINE

On Church Membership

Jesus Loves the Church and So Should You: Studies in Biblical Churchmanship by Earl M. Blackburn

Church Membership: How the World Knows Who Represents Jesus by Jonathan Leeman

Nine Marks of a Healthy Church by Mark Dever

On Meditating on God's Word, Prayer, and Other Spiritual Disciplines

Reading the Bible Supernaturally: Seeing and Savoring the Glory of God in Scripture by John Piper

Spiritual Disciplines for the Christian Life by Donald Whitney

Disciplines of a Godly Man by R. Kent Hughes

NOTES

Introduction

1. Jason Wilson, *Cry like a Man: Fighting for Freedom from Emotional Incarceration* (Colorado Springs, CO: David C. Cook, 2019), 19.

2. Wilson, *Cry like a Man*, 19.

3. "By this he means that, whenever the word of God is exhibited to us, he opens his bosom to us with maternal kindness, and, not satisfied with this, condescends to the humble affection of *a hen* watching over her *chickens*. Hence it follows, that our obstinacy is truly monstrous, if we do not permit him to *gather us together*." John Calvin and William Pringle, *Commentary on a Harmony of the Evangelists Matthew, Mark, and Luke* (Bellingham, WA: Logos Bible Software, 2010), 107.

4. Justin Ariel Bailey, *Interpreting Your World: Five Lenses for Engaging Theology and Culture* (Grand Rapids, MI: Baker Academic, 2022), 83.

5. This insight comes from Tim Chester, *A Meal with Jesus: Discovering Grace, Community, and Mission around the Table*, Re:Lit Series (Wheaton, IL: Crossway, 2011).

6. Edward Mote, "My Hope Is Built on Nothing Less," 1834, public domain.

Chapter 1

1. John W. Kleinig, *Wonderfully Made: A Protestant Theology of the Body* (Bellingham, WA: Lexham Press, 2021), 3.

2. If you are looking for a book that deals with the current debate about sexuality in our society, check out my book, *Known for Love: Loving Our LGBTQ Friends and Family without Compromising Biblical Truth* (Chicago: Moody Publishers, 2024).

3. Timothy C. Tennent, *For the Body: Recovering a Theology of Gender, Sexuality, and the Human Body* (Grand Rapids, MI: Zondervan Reflective, 2020), 8.

4. John Goldingay, *Old Testament Theology*, (Downers Grove, IL: IVP Academic, 2015), 42.

5. C. S. Lewis, *The Weight of Glory: And Other Addresses* (San Francisco: Harper, 2005).

6. John Calvin, *Institutes of the Christian Religion*, vols. 1 and 2, ed. John T. McNeill, trans. Ford Lewis Battles, vol. 1 of *The Library of Christian Classics* (Louisville, KY: Westminster John Knox, 2011), 183.

7. Calvin, *Institutes of the Christian Religion*, 184.

8. John Calvin and John King, *Commentary on the First Book of Moses Called Genesis* (Bellingham, WA: Logos Bible Software, 2010), 112.

9. Tennett, *For the Body*, 9.

10. Gregory of Nyssa, as quoted in Andrew Louth and Marco Conti, eds., *Genesis 1–11*, Ancient Christian Commentary on Scripture (Downers Grove, IL: InterVarsity Press, 2001), 51.

11. Charles Sherlock, *The Doctrine of Humanity, ed. Gerald Bray, Contours of Christian Theology* (Downers Grove, IL: InterVarsity Press, 1996), 198.

12. Victor P. Hamilton, *The Book of Genesis, Chapters 1–17*, The New International Commentary on the Old Testament (Grand Rapids, MI: Eerdmans, 1990), 241.

13. Oswald Chambers, Our Daily Bread Ministries, 20 February 2023, https://ourdailybread.org/article/the-delight-of-sacrifice/.

Chapter 2

1. Jason Wilson, *Cry like a Man: Fighting for Freedom from Emotional Incarceration*, 1st ed. (Colorado Springs, CO: David C Cook, 2019), 20.

2. Benjamin B. Warfield, *The Person and Work of Christ*, ed. Samuel G. Craig (Phillipsburg: P&R Publishing, 1950), 93.

3. Stephen J. Wellum, *God the Son Incarnate: The Doctrine of Christ*, Foundations of Evangelical Theology (Wheaton, IL: Crossway, 2016), 213.

4. Benjamin L. Merkle, "Ephesians," in *Ephesians–Philemon*, ed. Iain M. Duguid, James M. Hamilton Jr., and Jay Sklar, vol. XI of ESV Expository Commentary (Wheaton, IL: Crossway, 2018), 83.

5. John Stott, as quoted in Merkle, "Ephesians," 83.

6. BDAG, s.v. "πάθος," 748.

7. John Newton, "Amazing Grace," 1779, public domain.

Chapter 3

1. Daniel R. George, et al., "Perceptions of Diseases of Despair by Members of Rural and Urban High-Prevalence Communities," *JAMA Network Open* 4, no. 7 (July 23, 2021): e2118134, https://doi.org/10.1001/jamanetworkopen.2021.18134.

2. Edward T. Welch, *Depression: Looking up from the Stubborn Darkness* (Greensboro, NC: New Growth Press, 2011).

3. These descriptions are compiled by Welch, *Depression*.

4. Edward T. Welch, *Depression: Looking up from the Stubborn Darkness* (Greensboro, NC: New Growth Press, 2011); David P. Murray, *Reset: Living a Grace-Paced Life in a Burnout Culture* (Wheaton, IL: Crossway, 2017). What is in this section is the author's pastoral reflections and applications for men based on the wisdom mentioned in these books.

5. Leonard Ravenhill, *Why Revival Tarries* (Minneapolis, MN: Bethany, 2004), 25.

6. Welch, *Depression*.

Chapter 4

1. Victor P. Hamilton, *The Book of Genesis, Chapters 18–50*, New International Commentary on the Old Testament (Grand Rapids, MI: Eerdmans, 1995), 181.

2. While some attempt to argue that Paul is referring to a water baptism, given the relationship of this verse to the language of Romans 6 and its connection to the clear metaphor of being "clothed with Christ," it is best to understanding that Paul is using "baptism" as a metaphor for conversion. Paul uses the metaphor in a similar way in Romans 6:3–4, when he writes, "Or don't you know that all of us who were baptized into Christ Jesus were baptized into his death? We were therefore buried with him through baptism into death in order that, just as Christ was raised from the dead through the glory of the Father, we too may live a new life" (NIV).

Chapter 5

1. Miles Van Pelt, "3 Things You Should Know about the Song of Solomon," Ligonier Ministries, September 8, 2023, https://www.ligonier.org/learn/articles/3-things-song-of-solomon.

2. Casey Hough, "Who Were the Nephilim in Genesis 6?," Casey B. Hough (blog), January 6, 2020, https://www.caseyhough.com/who-were-the-nephilim-in-genesis-6.

3. For a more exhaustive list, see Daniel R. Heimbach, *True Sexual Morality: Recovering Biblical Standards for a Culture in Crisis* (Wheaton, IL: Crossway Books, 2004), 177.

4. Some point to 1 Corinthians 7:8–9 at this point, but we need to be mindful of the various interpretations in Christian history over this passage. There is some debate on whether Paul was always single or a widower. On the interpretation of Paul's words in 1 Corinthians 7:8–9, I find Calvin's explanation helpful. He writes, "The sum is this, that an unmarried life has many advantages, and that these are not to be despised, provided everyone measures himself according to his own size and measure. Hence, though virginity should be extolled even to the third heavens, this, at the same time, always remains true—that it does not suit all, but only those who have a special *gift* from God." John Calvin and John Pringle, *Commentaries on the Epistles of Paul the Apostle to the Corinthians* (Bellingham, WA: Logos Bible Software, 2010), 234.

5. See "Brothers, We Must Not Mind a Little Suffering," *Desiring God*, April 15, 1989, https://www.desiringgod.org/messages/brothers-we-must-not-mind-a-little-suffering.

6. Jesus participates in a cosmic wedding as the bridegroom for his church. The point I'm making here is that He was not married like, for instance, the apostle Peter was.

7. Timothy C. Tennent, *For the Body: Recovering a Theology of Gender, Sexuality, and the Human Body* (Grand Rapids, MI: Zondervan Reflective, 2020).

8. Oliver O'Donovan, "Transsexualism and Christian Marriage," *The Journal of Religious Ethics* 11, no. 1 (1983): 150.

9. Nancy Pearcey, *Love Thy Body: Answering Hard Questions about Life and Sexuality* (Grand Rapids, MI: Baker Books, 2018), 127.

10. Pearcey, *Love Thy Body*, 27.

11. Tim Keller with Kathy Keller, *The Meaning of Marriage: Facing the Complexities of Commitmnt with the Wisdom of God* (New York: Penguin, 2013). Also see Pearcey, *Love Thy Body*. Nancy Pearcey's writing on this subject was an influence on me and how I thought about this topic.

12. Anne Maloney, as quoted in Pearcey, *Love Thy Body*.

13. On the brain science, see William M. Struthers, *Wired for Intimacy: How Pornography Hijacks the Male Brain* (Downers Grove, IL: IVP Books, 2009).

14. This information is based on conversations the author had with single men while counseling them as their pastor.

15. Samuel L. Perry and Cyrus Schleifer, "Till Porn Do Us Part? A Longitudinal Examination of Pornography Use and Divorce," *The Journal of Sex Research* 55, no. 3 (March 24, 2018): 284–96, https://doi.org/10.1080/00224499.2017.1317709.

16. Simone Kühn and Jürgen Gallinat, "Brain Structure and Functional Connectivity Associated with Pornography Consumption: The Brain on Porn," *JAMA Psychiatry* 71, no. 7 (July 1, 2014): 827–34, https://doi.org/10.1001/jamapsychiatry.2014.93.

17. Casey Hough, "The Penalty of Pornography and the Power of the Gospel," Ethics and Religious Liberty Commission, January 5, 2017, https://erlc.com/resource/the-penalty-of-pornography-and-the-power-of-the-gospel.

Chapter 6

1. D. A. Carson, *A Call to Spiritual Reformation: Priorities from Paul and His Prayers* (Grand Rapids, MI: Baker Academic, rep. ed. 1992).

Chapter 7

1. John Piper, *When I Don't Desire GOD: How to Fight for Joy*, Tenth-anniversary edition (Wheaton IL: Crossway, 2013). I wanted to acknowledge his influence from this resource.

2. Paul Gardner, *1 Corinthians*, ed. Clinton E. Arnold, Zondervan Exegetical Commentary on the New Testament (Grand Rapids, MI: Zondervan, 2018), 411.

3. If you are not sure what I mean by a "good, biblically faithful local church," then I recommend checking out this short book by Mark Dever, *What Is a Healthy Church?*, 9Marks (Wheaton, IL: Crossway Books, 2007).

4. I'll mention a little more about the role local churches play in terms of accountability later in the chapter.

5. If you opt for a study Bible, just be aware that the notes in those Bibles are not authoritative and sometimes get things wrong. You will need to be discerning as you read study notes and make sure that Scripture is actually saying what others claim it is saying. As Christians, we believe Scripture alone is the supreme authority in the life of the believer and the church.

6. John Piper, "The American Revival of 1905," *Desiring God* (blog), September 14, 1987, https://www.desiringgod.org/articles/the-american-revival-of-1905.

ABOUT THE AUTHOR

Casey B. Hough (PhD, New Orleans Baptist Theological Seminary) currently serves as director of partnerships and curriculum at World Hope Ministries International and assistant professor of Biblical Interpretation at Luther Rice College & Seminary. Before moving to World Hope, Casey served in pastoral ministry for seventeen years. He and his wife, Hannah, have five children and live in Houston, Texas. You can learn more about Casey at his website, http://www.CaseyHough.com, where he maintains a weekly newsletter and podcast aimed at equipping the church with biblical resources for everyday life.